OUTBACK AUSTRALIA

ROAD TRIPS

This edition written and researched by

Anthony Ham

HOW TO USE THIS BOOK

Reviews

In the Destinations section:

All reviews are ordered in our authors' preference, starting with their most preferred option. Additionally:

Sights are arranged in the geographic order that we suggest you visit them and, within this order, by author preference.

Eating and Sleeping reviews are ordered by price range (budget, midrange, top end) and, within these ranges, by author preference.

Map Legend

Routes
- Trip Route
- Trip Detour
- Linked Trip
- Walk Route
- Tollway
- Freeway
- Primary
- Secondary
- Tertiary
- Lane
- Unsealed Road
- Plaza/Mall
- Steps
- Tunnel
- Pedestrian Overpass
- Walk Track/Path

Boundaries
- International
- State
- Cliff
- Wall

Population
- Capital (National)
- Capital (State)
- City/Large Town
- Town/Village

Transport
- Airport
- Cable Car/ Funicular
- Parking
- Train/Railway
- Tram
- Underground Train Station

Trips
- 1 Trip Numbers
- 9 Trip Stop
- Walking tour
- Trip Detour

Route Markers
- M31 1 National Highway
- A5 63 State Route

Hydrography
- River/Creek
- Intermittent River
- Swamp/Mangrove
- Canal
- Water
- Dry/Salt/ Intermittent Lake
- Glacier

Areas
- Beach
- Cemetery (Christian)
- Cemetery (Other)
- Park
- Forest
- Urban Area
- Sportsground

Note: Not all symbols shown here appear on the maps in this book

Symbols In This Book

- Top Tips
- Link Your Trips
- Tips from Locals
- Trip Detour
- History & Culture
- Family
- Food & Drink
- Outdoors
- Essential Photo
- Walking Tour
- Eating
- Sleeping

- Sights
- Beaches
- Activities
- Courses
- Tours
- Festivals & Events
- Sleeping
- Eating
- Drinking
- Entertainment
- Shopping
- Information & Transport

These symbols and abbreviations give vital information for each listing:

- Telephone number
- Opening hours
- Parking
- Nonsmoking
- Air-conditioning
- Internet access
- Wi-fi access
- Swimming pool
- Vegetarian selection
- English-language menu
- Family-friendly
- Pet-friendly
- Bus
- Ferry
- Tram
- Train

apt apartments
d double rooms
dm dorm beds
q quad rooms
r rooms
s single rooms
ste suites
tr triple rooms
tw twin rooms

CONTENTS

PLAN YOUR TRIP

ROAD TRIPS

DESTINATIONS

DRIVING IN AUSTRALIA..... 114

Above Kings Canyon (p56)

WELCOME TO OUTBACK AUSTRALIA

The outback, the Top End, the Red Centre. Whatever you call it, outback Australia has an elemental feel to it. It's here that so many Aussie landmarks of international repute reside, from Uluru, Kata Tjuta (the Olgas) and Kings Canyon in the centre, Katherine and Darwin to the north, Coober Pedy to the south and Lake Mungo in outback New South Wales.

As you'd expect from a predominantly outback region, the roads here can be empty, the distances are immense, and some northern trails may be impassable in the Big Wet (November to March). But the rewards are simply extraordinary, primary among them some of the best opportunities to experience this ancient land alongside its original inhabitants. Stock up on supplies and hit the road.

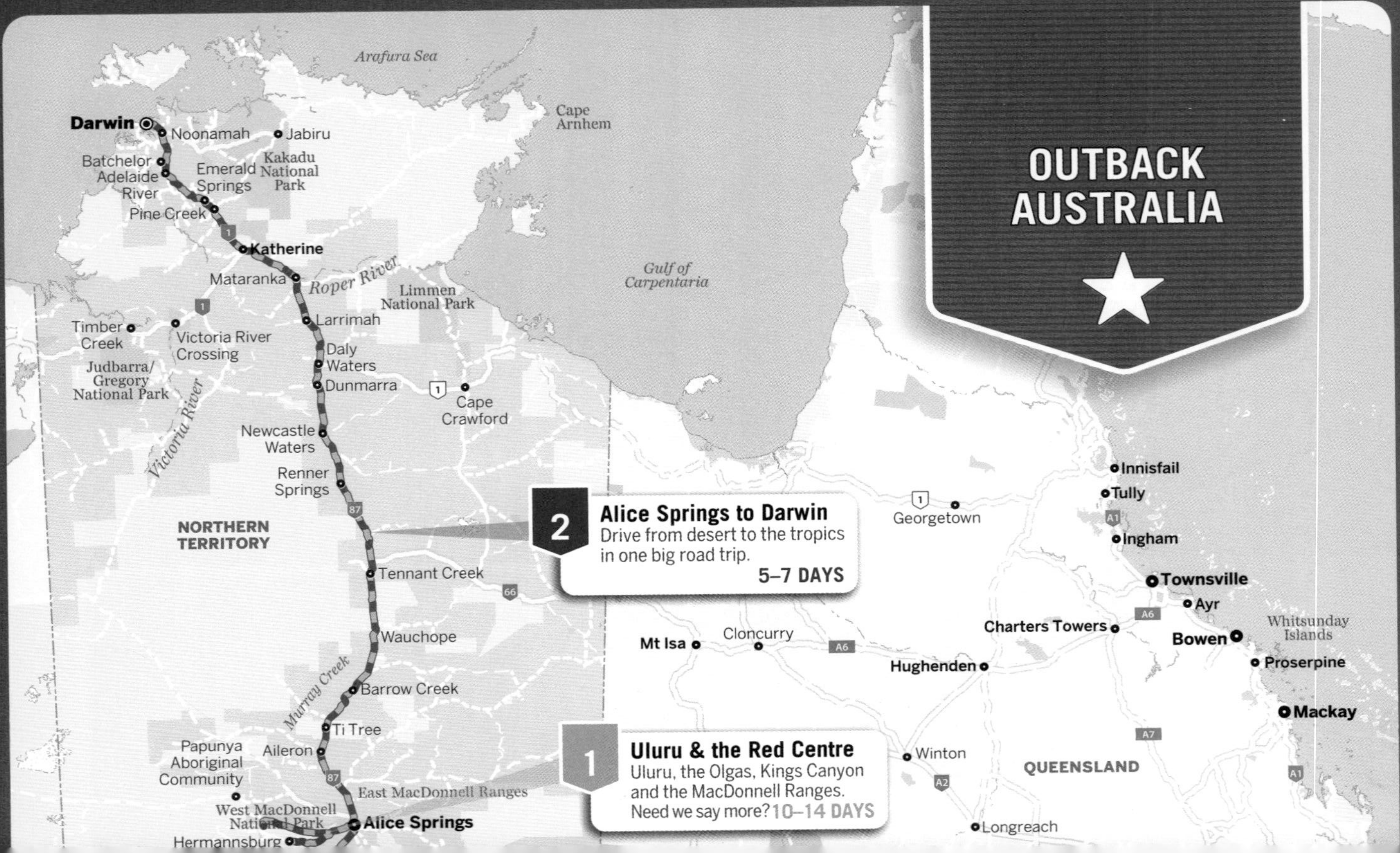

OUTBACK AUSTRALIA
2
Alice Springs to Darwin
Drive from desert to the tropics in one big road trip.
5–7 DAYS
1
Uluru & the Red Centre
Uluru, the Olgas, Kings Canyon and the MacDonnell Ranges. Need we say more?
10–14 DAYS
Arafura Sea
Gulf of Carpentaria
Cape Arnhem
Darwin
Noonamah
Jabiru
Batchelor
Adelaide River
Emerald Springs
Kakadu National Park
Pine Creek
Katherine
Mataranka
Roper River
Limmen National Park
Larrimah
Timber Creek
Victoria River Crossing
Judbarra/Gregory National Park
Daly Waters
Dunmarra
Cape Crawford
Victoria River
Newcastle Waters
Renner Springs
NORTHERN TERRITORY
Tennant Creek
Wauchope
Murray Creek
Barrow Creek
Ti Tree
Papunya Aboriginal Community
Aileron
East MacDonnell Ranges
West MacDonnell National Park
Alice Springs
Hermannsburg
Georgetown
Innisfail
Tully
Ingham
Townsville
Ayr
Mt Isa
Cloncurry
Charters Towers
Bowen
Whitsunday Islands
Hughenden
Proserpine
Mackay
Winton
QUEENSLAND
Longreach

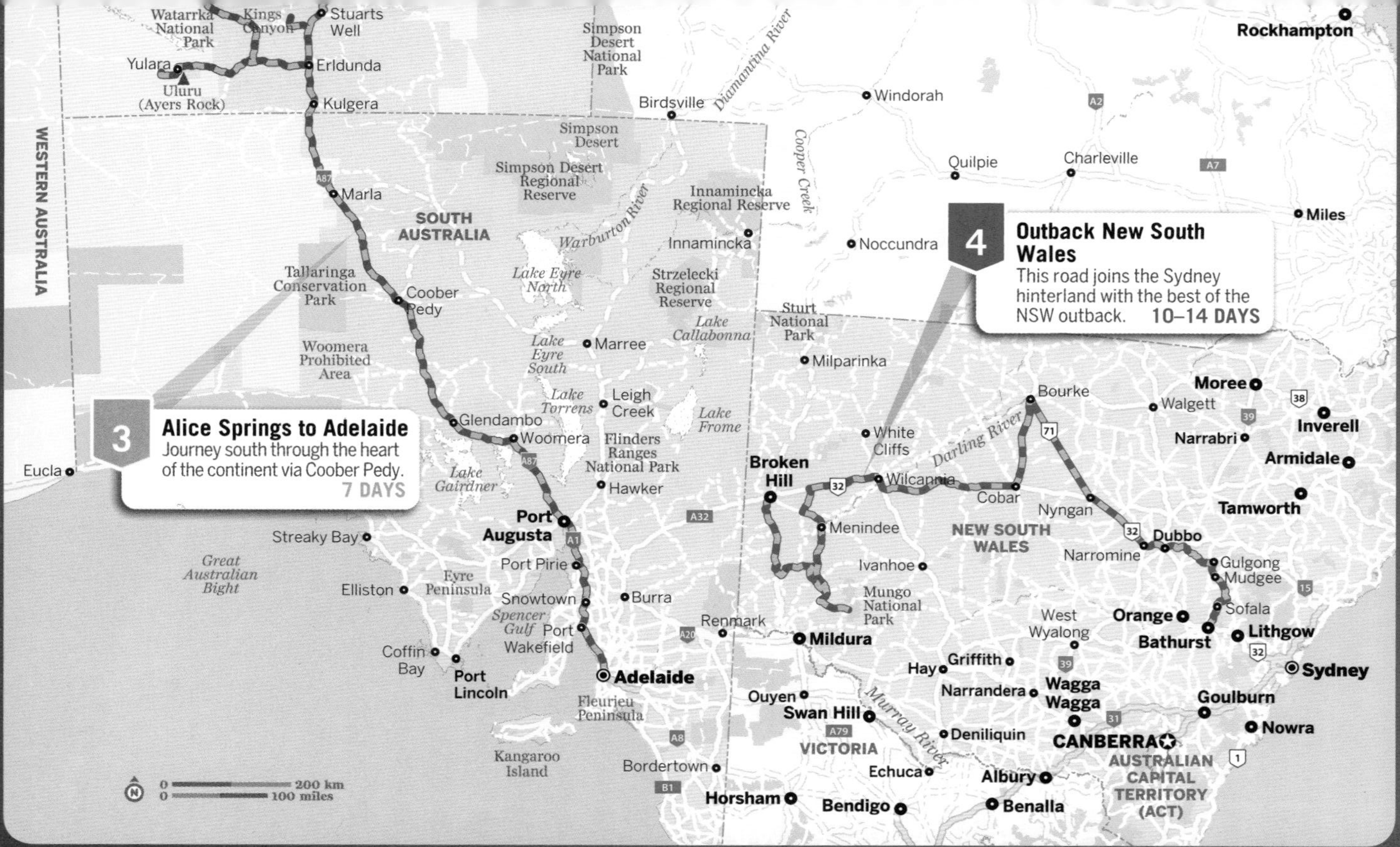

3
Alice Springs to Adelaide
Journey south through the heart of the continent via Coober Pedy.
7 DAYS
4
Outback New South Wales
This road joins the Sydney hinterland with the best of the NSW outback.
10–14 DAYS
WESTERN AUSTRALIA
SOUTH AUSTRALIA
NEW SOUTH WALES
VICTORIA
AUSTRALIAN CAPITAL TERRITORY (ACT)
Watarrka National Park
Kings Canyon
Stuarts Well
Yulara
Uluru (Ayers Rock)
Erldunda
Kulgera
Marla
Tallaringa Conservation Park
Coober Pedy
Woomera Prohibited Area
Glendambo
Woomera
Eucla
Lake Gairdner
Port Augusta
Streaky Bay
Great Australian Bight
Elliston
Eyre Peninsula
Port Pirie
Snowtown
Spencer Gulf
Port Wakefield
Coffin Bay
Port Lincoln
Adelaide
Fleurieu Peninsula
Kangaroo Island
Bordertown
Horsham
Simpson Desert National Park
Birdsville
Diamantina River
Simpson Desert
Simpson Desert Regional Reserve
Warburton River
Lake Eyre North
Lake Eyre South
Marree
Lake Torrens
Leigh Creek
Flinders Ranges National Park
Hawker
Burra
Renmark
Innamincka Regional Reserve
Innamincka
Strzelecki Regional Reserve
Lake Callabonna
Lake Frome
Cooper Creek
Sturt National Park
Milparinka
Windorah
Quilpie
Charleville
Noccundra
Rockhampton
Miles
White Cliffs
Broken Hill
Wilcannia
Darling River
Menindee
Ivanhoe
Mungo National Park
Mildura
Ouyen
Swan Hill
Murray River
Echuca
Bendigo
Bourke
Cobar
Nyngan
Dubbo
Narromine
Gulgong
Mudgee
Sofala
Orange
Bathurst
Lithgow
West Wyalong
Hay
Griffith
Narrandera
Wagga Wagga
Deniliquin
Albury
Benalla
CANBERRA
Goulburn
Nowra
Sydney
Moree
Walgett
Narrabri
Inverell
Armidale
Tamworth
A1
A2
A7
A8
A20
A32
A79
A87
B1
1
15
31
32
38
39
71
0 200 km
0 100 miles

OUTBACK AUSTRALIA HIGHLIGHTS

BETHUNE CARMICHAEL/GETTY IMAGES ©

BJORN HOLLAND/GETTY IMAGES ©

PAUL SINCLAIR PHOTOGRAPHY/GETTY IMAGES ©

Uluru-Kata Tjuta National Park (left) Nothing prepares you for the burnished grandeur of Uluru as it first appears on the outback horizon. With its remote desert location, deep cultural significance and dazzling natural beauty, Uluru is a pilgrimage of sorts. See it on Trip 1

Devil's Marbles (above) Mysterious remote boulders by the roadside. See them on Trip 2

Mungo National Park (right) Ancient wind-sculpted land in southeast New South Wales. See it on Trip 4

CITY GUIDE

Mung bean biscuits, Nightcliff Market (p84)

DARWIN

The cosmopolitan capital of Darwin is Australia's doorway to Asia and celebrates its multicultural mix with delicious fusion cuisine and a relaxed tropical vibe. Darwin feels more like a big town than a city, and the dreamy coastline around its outer reaches rakes at the heart when a blood red sun is dipping over the horizon.

Getting Around

Darwin is relatively compact, but having your own car is particularly useful for visiting the markets in the northern suburbs and the parks on the city's fringe. Central Darwin and the Waterfront Precinct are easily walkable.

Parking

Darwin's CBD has paid parking meters; the cost ranges between $1.20 and $2.40 per hour, depending on location. There is free overnight parking in the majority of off-street car parks. See the Darwin City website (www.darwin.nt.gov.au) for specifics.

Where to Eat

The Darwin Waterfront Precinct is a great spot for a lovely dinner of fresh seafood with a variety of options to suit all budgets. Food at Parap Village Market is also a highlight – arrive hungry!

Where to Stay

Darwin has a good range of sleeping options, mostly clustered near the CBD. Hostels are generally concentrated in a bar-heavy stretch of Mitchell St. There are a few decent camping/caravan options within 10km of the city. Darwin's larger hotels quote inflated rack rates but there are good specials to be found online.

Useful Websites

City of Darwin
(www.darwin.nt.gov.au)

Tourism NT
(www.travelnt.com)

Tourism Top End
(www.tourismtopend.com.au)

Road Trip Through Darwin: 2

Destination coverage: p75

Adelaide's Central Market (p93)

ADELAIDE

Relax after your epic drive with a few days in gracious, relaxed Adelaide. Capital of the driest state on the driest inhabited continent, Adelaide beats the heat by celebrating life's finer things: fine landscapes, fine festivals, fine food and (...OK, forget the other three) fine wine.

Getting Around

Adelaide is pancake flat – perfect for walking or cycling (if it's not too hot!). Buses, trains and trams also service the city; **Adelaide Metro** (www.adelaidemetro.com.au) has information and sells tickets.

Parking

Parking is cheap and plentiful throughout the city. Hotel parking sometimes incurs an additional fee.

Where to Eat

Those in the know head to West End hotspots such as Gouger St, Chinatown and food-filled Central Market.

Where to Stay

Most of Adelaide's budget accommodation is in the city centre but in a city this easy to get around, staying outside the CBD is viable. For beachside accommodation, try Glenelg.

Useful Websites

South Australian Visitor Information Centre (www.southaustralia.com) Info on Adelaide and South Australia.

Road Trip Through Adelaide: 4

Destination coverage: p92

NEED TO KNOW

MOBILE PHONES

European phones work on Australia's network, but most American and Japanese phones won't. Use global roaming or a local SIM card and prepaid account. Telstra has the widest coverage.

INTERNET ACCESS

Wi-fi is widespread in urban areas, less so in remote Australia. For public wi-fi locations, visit www.freewifi.com.au. There are relatively few internet cafes; try public libraries.

FUEL

Unleaded and diesel fuel widely available. Prices vary from $1.20 in cities to $2.20 in the outback. Distances between fill-ups can be long in the outback.

RENTAL CARS

Avis (www.avis.com.au)

Budget (www.budget.com.au)

Europcar (www.europcar.com.au)

Hertz (www.hertz.com.au)

IMPORTANT NUMBERS

Emergencies ☎000

International Access Code ☎0011

Climate

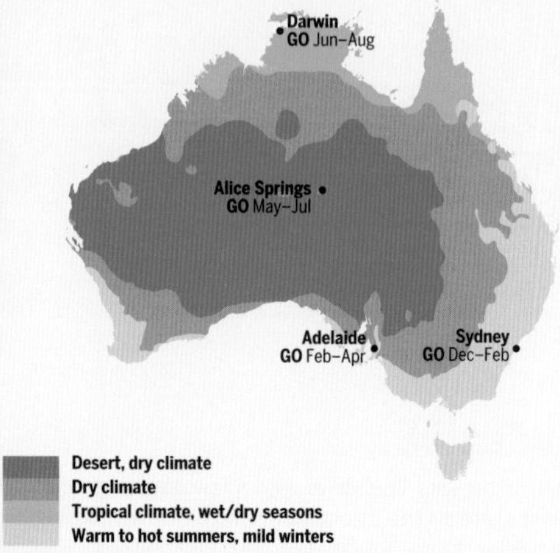

When to Go

High Season (Dec–Feb)

» Summertime: local holidays, busy beaches and cricket.

» Prices rise 25% for big-city accommodation.

» Wet (and hence low) season in northern Western Australia, Northern Territory and northern Queensland.

Shoulder Season (Mar–May & Sep–Nov)

» Warm sun, clear skies, shorter queues.

» Easter (late March or early April) is busy with Aussie families on the loose.

» Autumn leaves are atmospheric in Victoria, Tasmania and South Australia.

Low Season (Jun–Aug)

» Cool rainy days down south; mild days and sunny skies up north.

» Low tourist numbers; attractions keep slightly shorter hours.

» Head for the desert, the tropical north or the snow.

Daily Costs

Budget: Less than $100

» Hostel dorm bed: $25–35 a night

» Simple pizza or pasta meal: $10–15

» Short bus or tram ride: $4

Midrange: $100–$280

» Double room in a motel, B&B or hotel: $100–200

» Breakfast or lunch in a cafe: $20–40

» Short taxi ride: $25

Top End: More than $280

» Double room in a top-end hotel: from $200

» Three-course meal in a classy restaurant: $80

» Nightclub cover charge: $10–20

Eating

Cafes Good for breakfasts and light lunches.

Restaurants International and mod-Oz cuisine.

Pubs Well-priced bistro food.

Roadhouses No-nonsense outback meals.

Vegetarians Wide choice in cities, less so elsewhere.

Eating price indicators represent the cost of a standard main course:

$	less than $15
$$	$15 to $32
$$$	more than $32

Sleeping

B&Bs Often in restored heritage buildings.

Campgrounds & Caravan Parks Most have sites and simple cabins.

Hostels Buzzing budget digs with dorm beds.

Hotels From simple to upmarket.

Motels No-frills but fine for a night.

Sleeping price indicators represent the cost of a double room with private bathroom in high season. Sydney, Perth and parts of northern Western Australia will cost more:

$	less than $100
$$	$100 to $200
$$$	more than $200

Arriving in Australia

Sydney Airport

Bus Pre-arranged shuttle buses service city hotels.

Train AirportLink trains run to the city centre every 10 minutes from around 5am to 1am (20 minutes).

Taxi A taxi into the city costs $40 to $50 (30 minutes).

Melbourne Airport

Bus SkyBus services (24-hour) run to the city (20 minutes), leaving every 10 to 30 minutes.

Taxi A taxi into the city costs around $40 (25 minutes).

Brisbane Airport

Bus Shuttle buses service city hotels (bookings required).

Train Airtrain trains run into the city centre (20 minutes) every 15 to 30 minutes from 5am (6am weekends) to 10pm.

Taxi A taxi into the city costs $35 to $45 (25 minutes).

Money

ATMs are widespread, but not off the beaten track or in some small towns. Visa and MasterCard are widely accepted, Diners Club and Amex less so.

Tipping

It's common (but not obligatory) to tip in restaurants if the service warrants it; 5% to 10% is the norm. Round up taxi fares.

Opening Hours

Banks 9.30am-4pm Monday to Thursday, until 5pm Friday

Cafes 7am-4pm or 5pm

Petrol stations & roadhouses 8am-10pm

Pubs noon-2pm and 6-9pm (food); drinking hours are longer and continue into the evening, especially from Thursday to Saturday

Restaurants noon-2pm and 6-9pm

Shops 10am-5pm or 6pm Monday to Friday, until either noon or 5pm on Saturday and (in major cities and tourist towns) Sunday

For more, see Driving in Australia (p112).

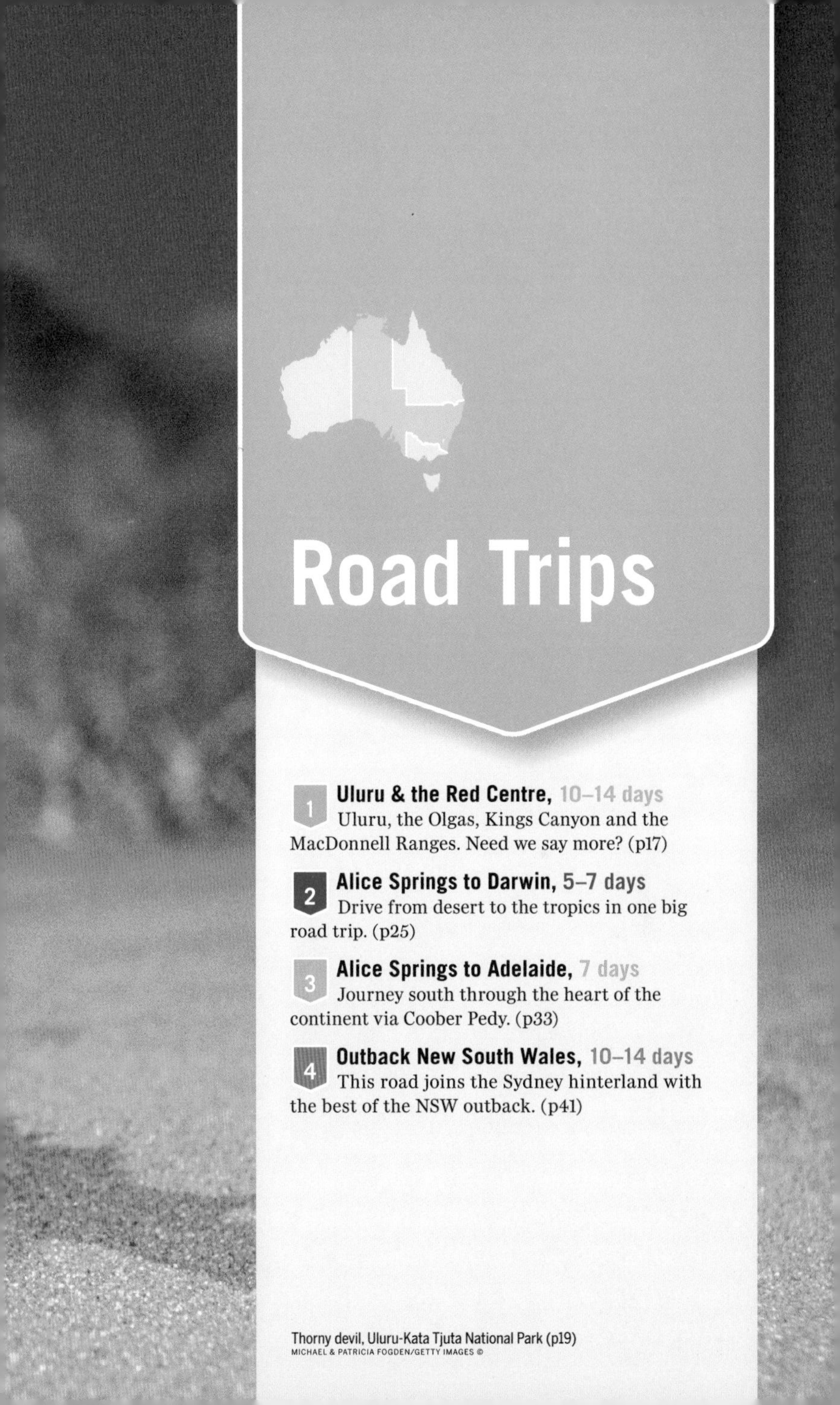

Road Trips

Thorny devil, Uluru-Kata Tjuta National Park (p19)

Uluru & the Red Centre

1

Welcome to Australia's Red Centre, home to the country's most magnificent and utterly unforgettable outback landmarks – Uluru, the Olgas, Kings Canyon and the MacDonnell Ranges.

TRIP HIGHLIGHTS

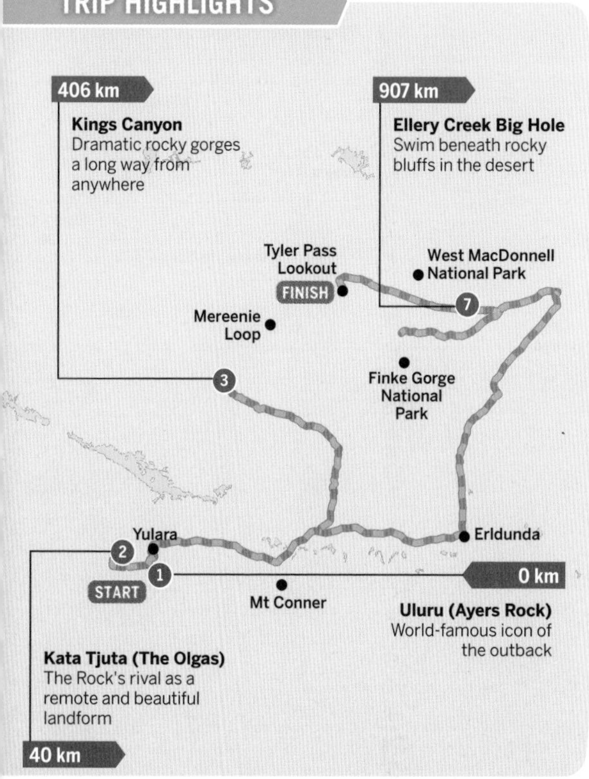

10–14 DAYS
1224KM / 761 MILES

GREAT FOR...

BEST TIME TO GO

April to August has cooler temperatures; it's fiercely hot September to March.

ESSENTIAL PHOTO

Sunset at Uluru.

BEST FOR OUTDOORS

Walk through the Valley of the Winds for true outback magic.

Left Uluru (Ayers Rock; p19)

1 Uluru & the Red Centre

If you make one trip into the Australian outback, make it this one. Uluru is an extraordinary, soulful place utterly unlike anywhere else on the planet. Nearby, Kata Tjuta (the Olgas) and Kings Canyon leave spellbound all who visit, while the West MacDonnell Ranges capture the essence of the Red Centre – red earth, red rocks and ghostly gums in a spiritually charged landscape.

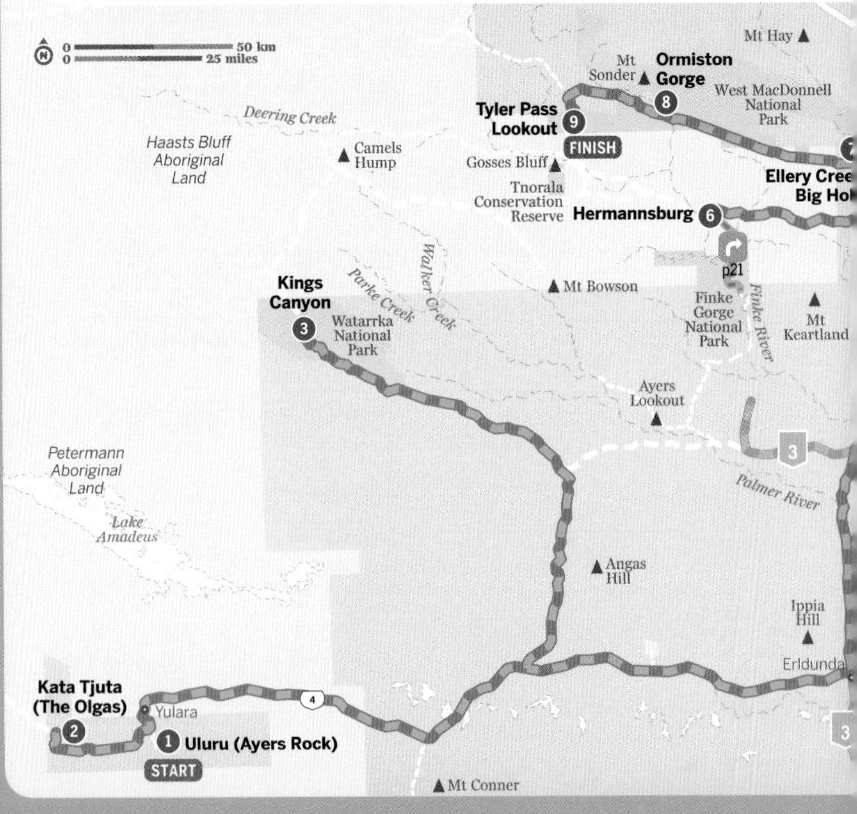

TRIP HIGHLIGHT

❶ Uluru (Ayers Rock; p50)

Uluru: nothing can really prepare you for the immensity, grandeur, changing colour and stillness of 'the Rock'. The first sight of Uluru on the horizon invariably astounds even the most jaded traveller. Before arriving, 1km short of Uluru, visit the **Uluru-Kata Tjuta Cultural Centre** (☎08-8956 1128; www.parksaustralia.gov.au/uluru/do/cultural-centre.html; ⏰7am-6pm). Uluru itself is 3.6km long and rises a towering 348m from the surrounding sandy scrubland (867m above sea level). Closer inspection reveals a wondrous contoured surface concealing numerous sacred sites of particular significance to the Anangu. If your first sight of Uluru is during the afternoon, it appears as an ochre-brown colour, scored and pitted by dark shadows. As the sun sets, it illuminates the rock in burnished orange, then a series of deeper reds before it fades into charcoal. A performance in reverse, with marginally fewer spectators, is given at dawn. There's plenty to see and do: meandering walks, bike rides, guided tours, desert culture and simply contemplating the many changing colours and moods of the great monolith itself.

The Drive » The road from Uluru to Kata Tjuta (40km) is sealed, as is the 20km road between Uluru and Yulara (where all of the accommodation for both places is). There are no other roads out here: you can't get lost.

TRIP HIGHLIGHT

❷ Kata Tjuta (The Olgas; p54)

No journey to Uluru is complete without a visit to Kata Tjuta, part of **Uluru-Kata Tjuta National Park** (www.parksaustralia.gov.au/uluru/index.html; adult/child $25/free) and a striking group of domed rocks huddled together about 35km west of Uluru. There are 36 boulders shoulder to shoulder forming deep valleys and steep-sided gorges. Many visitors find them even more captivating than their prominent neighbour. The tallest rock, **Mt Olga** (546m; 1066m above sea level), is approximately 200m higher than Uluru. Kata Tjuta means 'many heads' and is of great *tjukurpa* (Aboriginal law, religion and custom) significance, particularly for men, so stick to the tracks. The

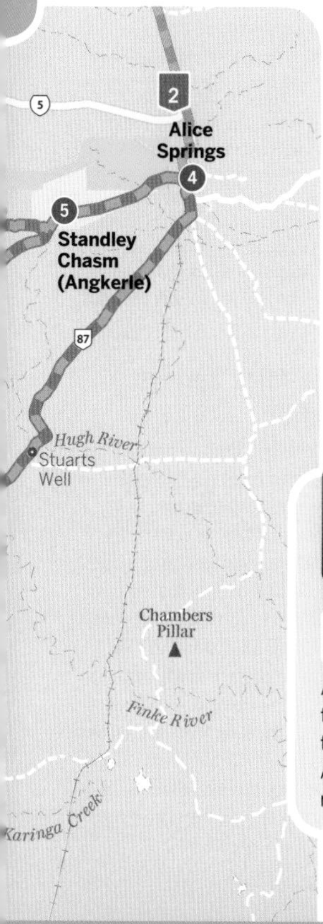

LINK YOUR TRIP

2 Alice Springs to Darwin

Alice Springs is Stop 4 on the Uluru & the Red Centre trip, and it's also where the Alice Springs to Darwin route (1493km) begins.

3 Alice Springs to Adelaide

From Alice Springs, the other choice is to head south to Adelaide (1500km).

7.4km **Valley of the Winds** loop (two to four hours) winds through the gorges, giving excellent views of the surreal domes. The short signposted track beneath towering rock walls into pretty **Walpa Gorge** (2.6km return, 45 minutes) is especially beautiful in the afternoon. Like Uluru, Kata Tjuta is at its glorious, blood-red best at sunset.

The Drive » From Kata Tjuta, return the 40km to Uluru, then 20km more to Yulara, before the long road really begins. The Lasseter Hwy runs east (watch for Mt Conner, the large mesa (table-top mountain) that looms 350m out of the desert away to the south). Some 137km from Yulara, take the Kings Canyon turn-off, from where you've 169km to go.

TRIP HIGHLIGHT

3 Kings Canyon (p56)

The yawning chasm of Kings Canyon in Watarrka National Park is one of the most spectacular sights in central Australia. This is one place where it pays to get out and walk, and you'll be rewarded with awesome views on the **Kings Canyon Rim Walk** (6km loop, four hours; you must begin before 9am on hot days), which many travellers rate as a highlight of their trip to the Centre. After a short but steep climb (the only 'difficult' part of the trail), the walk skirts the canyon's rim before descending down wooden stairs to the **Garden of Eden**: a lush pocket of ferns and prehistoric cycads around a tranquil pool. The next section of the trail winds through a swarm of giant beehive domes: weathered sandstone outcrops, which to the Luritja represent the men of the Kuniya Dreaming. If that all sounds like too much hard work, take a scenic helicopter flight with **Professional Helicopter Services** (PHS; ☎08-8956 2003; www.phs.com.au; flights per person $95-275) or **Kings Creek Helicopters** (☎08-8956 7474; www.kingscreekstation.com.au; flights per person $70-480).

The Drive » With a 4WD, it's a short hop to Hermannsburg, but otherwise, you'll need to return 169km to the Lasseter Hwy, travel 108km east to the Stuart Hwy, then 200km north and then northeast into Alice Springs – a very long day but the scenery has its own rewards.

4 Alice Springs (p60)

Alice Springs is many things to many people – rough-and-tumble frontier town, centre for Indigenous arts, set amid glorious outback scenery. They're all true, and yet sitting as it does in the approximate midpoint of this journey, its main appeal may lie in the chance to wash off the dust, sleep between clean sheets and keep at bay the great

MEREENIE LOOP ROAD

The Red Centre Way is the 'back road' from Alice to the Rock. It incorporates an 'inner loop' comprising Namatjira and Larapinta Drs, plus the rugged Mereenie Loop Rd, the short cut to Kings Canyon. This dusty, heavily corrugated road is not to be taken lightly, and hire car companies won't permit their 2WDs to be driven on it. There can be deep sandy patches and countless corrugations, depending on the time of year and how recently it's been graded. It's best travelled in a high-clearance vehicle, preferably a 4WD. Be aware that 2WD hire vehicles will not be covered by insurance on this road.

To travel along this route, which passes through Aboriginal land, you need a Mereenie Tour Pass ($5), which is valid for one day and includes a booklet with details about local Aboriginal culture and a route map. The pass is issued on the spot (usually only on the day of travel) at the visitor information centre in Alice Springs, Glen Helen Resort, Kings Canyon Resort and Hermannsburg service station.

emptiness for a night. To anchor your visit, take in the **Araluen Cultural Precinct** (☎08-8951 1122; http://artsandmuseums.nt.gov.au/araluen-cultural-precinct; cnr Larapinta Dr & Memorial Ave; precinct pass adult/child $15/10), Alice Springs' cultural hub.

The Drive » Heading west from Alice, 6km short of where the main Larapinta Dr splits, take the turn-off for Standley Chasm.

5 Standley Chasm (Angkerle)

With their stunning beauty and rich diversity of plants and animals, the West MacDonnell Ranges are not to be missed, and nowhere are they more beautiful than here. Spectacular **Standley Chasm** (☎08-8956 7440; adult/concession $10/8; ⏲8am-5pm, last chasm entry 4.30pm) is owned and run by the nearby community of Iwupataka. This narrow corridor slices neatly through the rocky range and in places the smooth walls rise to 80m. The rocky path into the gorge (20 minutes, 1.2km) follows a creek bed lined with ghost gums and cycads. You can continue to a second chasm (one hour return) or head up Larapinta Hill (45 minutes return) for a fine view.

The Drive » Six kilometres west of Standley Chasm, the road forks – take the left fork (Larapinta Dr) and follow the signs to Hermannsburg, 126km from the turn-off.

6 Hermannsburg

The Aboriginal community of Hermannsburg (Ntaria), about 125km from Alice Springs, is famous as the one-time home of artist Albert Namatjira and as the site of the **Hermannsburg Mission** (☎08-8956 7402; www.hermannsburg.com.au; adult/child $10/5; ⏲9am-5pm Mon-Sat, 10.30am-5pm Sun), whose whitewashed walls are shaded by majestic river gums and date palms. This fascinating monument to the Northern Territory's early Lutheran missionaries includes a school building, a church and various outbuildings. The 'Manse' houses an art gallery and a history of the life and times of Albert Namatjira, as well as works of 39 Hermannsburg artists. Just west of Hermannsburg is **Namatjira's House**.

The Drive » Return back to where the road forked, then turn hard left onto Namatjira Dr, which takes you to a whole series of gorges and gaps in the West MacDonnell Ranges. Ellery Creek Big Hole is 51km after you take the turn-off.

DETOUR: FINKE GORGE NATIONAL PARK

Start: 6 Hermannsburg

With its primordial landscape, the Finke Gorge National Park, south of Hermannsburg, is one of central Australia's premier wilderness reserves. The top attraction is **Palm Valley**, famous for its red cabbage palms, which exist nowhere else in the world. These relics from prehistoric times give the valley the feel of a picture-book oasis. Tracks include the **Arankaia walk** (2km loop, one hour), which traverses the valley, returning via the sandstone plateau; the **Mpulungkinya track** (5km loop, two hours), heading down the gorge before joining the Arankaia walk; and the **Mpaara track** (5km loop, two hours), taking in the Finke River, Palm Bend and a rugged natural amphitheatre (a semicircle of sandstone formations sculpted by a now-extinct meander of Palm Creek).

Access to the park follows the sandy bed of the Finke River and rocky tracks, and so a high-clearance 4WD is essential. If you don't have one, several tour operators go to Palm Valley from Alice Springs. The turn-off to Palm Valley starts about 1km west of the Hermannsburg turn-off on Larapinta Dr.

RICHARD I'ANSON/GETTY IMAGES ©

FRANCES ANDRIJICH/GETTY IMAGES ©

TRIP HIGHLIGHT

7 Ellery Creek Big Hole

Ellery Creek Big Hole is one of those fabulous outback miracles – a steep-sided rocky waterhole with a small, white-sand beach and hues of Red Centre red, deep waterhole blue and eucalyptus green. The large permanent waterhole is a popular place for a swim on a hot day (the water is usually *freezing*): there are no crocs lurking in the shallows...

The Drive » About 11km further, a rough gravel track leads to narrow, ochre-red Serpentine Gorge, which has a lovely waterhole, a lookout and ancient cycads. The Ochre Pits line a dry creek bed 11km west of Serpentine and were a source of pigment for Aboriginal people. Ormiston Gorge is 25km beyond the Ochre Pits.

8 Ormiston Gorge

Majestic Ormiston Gorge is the most impressive chasm in the West MacDonnells. There's a waterhole shaded with ghost gums, and the gorge curls around to the enclosed Ormiston Pound. It is a haven for

JIM HOLMES / DESIGN PICS/GETTY IMAGES ©

wildlife and you can expect to see some critters among the spinifex slopes and mulga woodland. There are walking tracks, including to the **Ghost Gum Lookout** (20 minutes), which affords brilliant views down the gorge, and the excellent, circuitous **Pound Walk** (three hours, 7.5km). There's a visitor centre, a kiosk and an enduring sense of peace whenever the tourist buses move on.

The Drive » About 2km beyond Ormiston Gorge is the turn-off to Glen Helen Gorge, where the Finke River cuts through the MacDonnells. Only 1km past Glen Helen is a good lookout over Mt Sonder. If you continue northwest for 25km you'll reach the turn-off (4WD only) to multihued, cathedral-like Redbank Gorge. The paved road ends at Tyler Pass.

9 Tyler Pass Lookout

There's something impossibly romantic (in a desert sense, at least) about reaching the end of the paved road, and here you are. Even where your view west is obscured by rolling sand hills, just knowing that the desert stretches out beyond here for thousands of kilometres is enough to produce a delicious sense of vertigo. Tyler Pass Lookout provides a dramatic view of Tnorala (Grosse Bluff), the legacy of an earth-shattering comet impact, but it's the end-of-the-earth, end-of-the-road sense that you'll remember most, long after you're home.

Top far left Kata Tjuta (The Olgas; p19)
Far left Aboriginal boy holding a joey
Left Kings Canyon (p20)

Alice Springs to Darwin

2

One of those great Aussie road trips that cuts through the heart of the continent, Alice Springs to Darwin takes you on a journey to remember.

TRIP HIGHLIGHTS

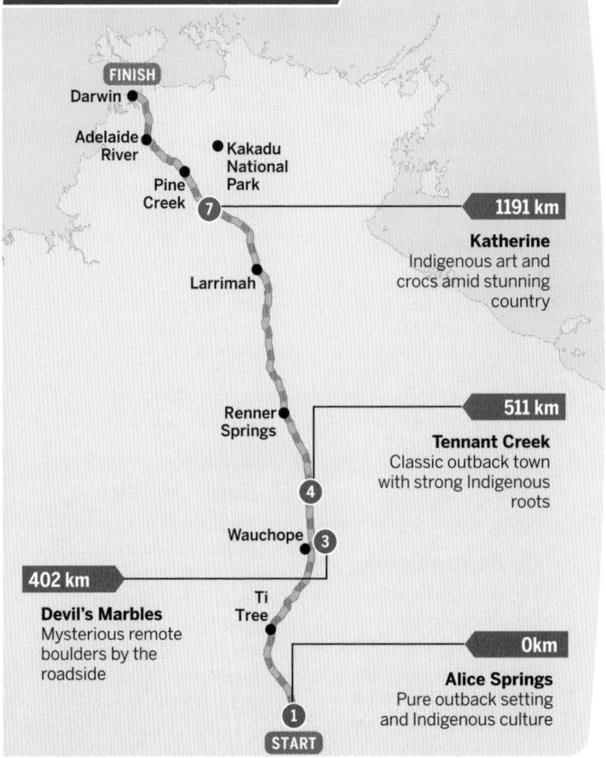

5–7 DAYS
1493KM / 928 MILES

GREAT FOR...

BEST TIME TO GO

April to October – the Big Wet ruins the rest of the year in the north.

ESSENTIAL PHOTO

Devil's Marbles for their sacred connotations and sheer beauty.

BEST FOR OUTDOORS

Go looking for crocs by night at Katherine.

Left Devil's Marbles (p26)

2 Alice Springs to Darwin

All the monotony and magnificence of the outback is on show on this long and lonely desert crossing. In Alice Springs, Tennant Creek and all the isolated homesteads and settlements in between, the air is tinder dry and the colours those of the desert. By Katherine, you're in a different world, where the outback meets the tropics, and the latter very much takes hold by the time you pull into Darwin.

TRIP HIGHLIGHT

1 Alice Springs (p57)

There's no town quite like Alice. Marooned in the heart of the outback, this ruggedly beautiful town is shaped by its mythical landscapes. The mesmerising MacDonnell Ranges stretch east and west from the town centre, and you don't have to venture far to find yourself among ochre-red gorges, pastel-hued hills and ghostly white gum trees. As much as the terrain, it's the Aboriginal character of Alice that sets it apart. Two excellent places to start your exploration of local Indigenous culture are the excursions run by **Emu Run Tours** (☎1800 687 220; www.emurun.com.au; 72 Todd St) and a visit to the excellent Araluen Cultural Precinct (p60).

The Drive » You've a very long road ahead of you, so getting an early start helps. Watch for fine views of the MacDonnell Ranges as you leave town, then barrel on up the dry and dusty highway for 135km to tiny Aileron – don't blink or you might just miss it – with another 149km into Barrow Creek.

2 Barrow Creek

The outback does a fine line in wonderfully offbeat personalities forged in the isolation afforded by this vast and empty land. Sometimes it's a person, at others a building. But just as often it's the sum total of these and all manner of passing wanderers. One such place is the rustic **Barrow Creek Hotel**, one of the highway's truly eccentric outback pubs. In the tradition of shearers who'd write their name on a banknote and pin it to the wall to ensure they could afford a drink when next they passed through, travellers continue to leave notes and photos, and the result is a priceless collage of outback life. Food and fuel are available and next door is one of the original Telegraph Stations on the Overland Telegraph Line. There ain't a whole lot more here, but you'll soon get used to that in these parts.

The Drive » It's 118km from Barrow Creek to the Devil's Marbles. At the kooky Wycliffe Well Roadhouse & Holiday Park, you can fill up with fuel and food or stay and spot UFOs that apparently fly over with astonishing regularity. At Wauchope (war-kup), 10km south of the Devil's Marbles, you'll pass the Wauchope Hotel, where you can stay if need be.

TRIP HIGHLIGHT

3 Devil's Marbles

The gigantic granite boulders piled in precarious piles beside the Stuart Hwy, 105km south of Tennant Creek, are known as the Devil's Marbles (or Karlu Karlu in the local Warumungu

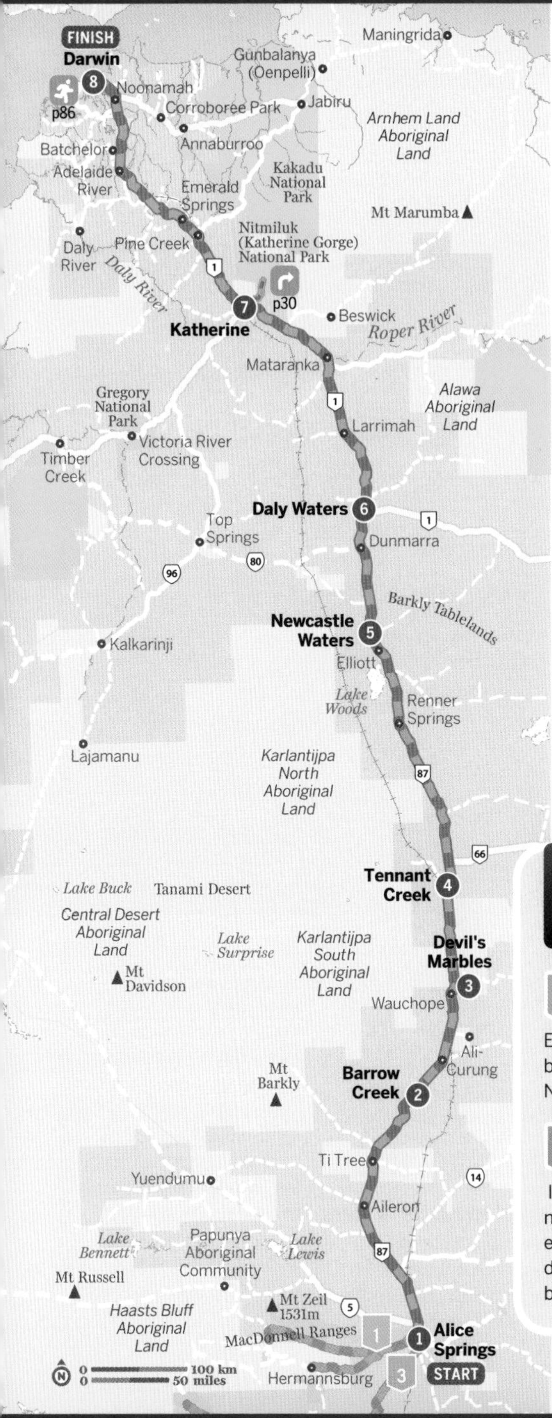

language) and they're one of the more beautiful sights along this road. The Marbles are a sacred site for the traditional Aboriginal owners of the land, for whom the rocks are, according to one story, believed to be the eggs of the Rainbow Serpent. Such are the extremes of temperature out here that the boulders undergo a constant 24-hour cycle of expansion and contraction, hence the large cracks in many of them.

The Drive » Unless you've slept somewhere along the way, the final 105km into Tennant Creek, 511km north of Alice, can't come quick enough. And after so long on the road, arriving feels even more like paradise thanks to its oasis-like lushness and abundant water.

LINK YOUR TRIP

1 Uluru & the Red Centre

Explore the grandeur and beauty of Uluru-Kata Tjuta National Park.

3 Alice Springs to Adelaide

Instead of heading north, head south. Works especially well if you've done Trip 2 in reverse and began in Darwin.

TRIP HIGHLIGHT

4 Tennant Creek (p70)

Tennant Creek is the only town of any size between Katherine, 680km to the north, and Alice Springs, 511km to the south, although it's all relative: just 3061 people lived here the last time the census-takers passed through. Fortunately, there's more than just a good meal, petrol and clean sheets to keep you occupied. Tennant Creek is known as Jurnkurakurr to the local Warumungu people (almost half of the town's population is of Aboriginal descent) and the innovative **Nyinkka Nyunyu** (☎08-8962 2699; www.nyinkkanyunyu.com.au; Paterson St; tour guide $15; ⏰9am-5pm Mon-Fri, 10am-2pm Sat & Sun Oct-Apr, 8am-6pm Mon-Sat, 10am-2pm Sun May-Sep) museum and gallery highlights their dynamic art and culture; learn about bush tucker and Dreaming stories with your personal guide. And to really get a personal experience of the area, take a **Kelly's Ranch** (☎08-8962 2045; www.kellysranch.com.au; 5 Fazaldeen Rd; trail rides per person $150, lesson per person $50) two-hour horse trail ride with local Warumungu man Jerry Kelly.

CREDIT/GETTY IMAGES ©

The Drive » Just 26km north of Tennant Creek you'll pass Three Ways, the junction of the Stuart and Barkly Hwys. Banka Banka, 100km north of Tennant Creek, has a mud-brick bar, while Renner Springs is generally accepted as the dividing line between the seasonally wet Top End and the dry Centre; there's a decent roadhouse.

5 Newcastle Waters

Most small outback settlements lead a fairly precarious existence and the line between survival and abandonment can be pretty tenuous. Many make it, but Newcastle Waters is an eerie example of those that don't. The surrounding station of the same name was (and remains) an important cattle station, but the town's role as a drovers' waystation was doomed once road and rail transport took over as the primary means of transport in the 1960s.

Katherine Gorge (p30)

These days it's a veritable ghost town, with atmospheric, historic timber-and-corrugated-iron buildings, including the Junction Hotel, cobbled together from abandoned windmills in 1932.

The Drive » From Newcastle Waters to Daly Waters, it's 132 dry and dusty kilometres. Just before Daly Waters, the sealed Carpentaria Hwy branches off to the east, bound for the Gulf of Carpentaria at Eadangula some 376km away.

6 Daly Waters (p71)

Most outback towns of any reasonable size have some unusual claim to fame; Daly Waters, about 3km off the highway, is no exception. Daly Waters was an important staging post in the early days of aviation – Amy Johnson landed here on her epic flight from England to Australia in 1930. Just about everyone stops at the famous **Daly Waters Pub** (08-8975 9927; www.dalywaterspub.com; unpowered/powered sites $16/28, d $70-110, cabins $135-175;). Decorated with business cards, bras, banknotes and memorabilia from passing

DETOUR: NITMILUK (KATHERINE GORGE) NATIONAL PARK

Start: 7 Katherine

Spectacular **Katherine Gorge** forms the backbone of the 2920-sq-km **Nitmiluk (Katherine Gorge) National Park** (www.parksandwildlife.nt.gov.au/parks/find/nitmiluk), about 30km from Katherine. A series of 13 deep sandstone **gorges** have been carved out by the **Katherine River** on its journey from Arnhem Land to the Timor Sea. It is a hauntingly beautiful place – though it can get crowded in peak season – and a must-do from Katherine. In the Dry the tranquil river is perfect for a paddle, but in the Wet the deep, still waters and dividing rapids are engulfed by an awesome torrent that churns through the gorge. Plan to spend at least a full day canoeing or cruising on the river and bushwalking. The traditional owners are the Jawoyn Aboriginal people who jointly manage Nitmiluk with Parks & Wildlife. **Nitmiluk Tours** (☎08-8972 1253, 1300 146 743; www.nitmiluktours.com.au) manages accommodation, cruises and activities within the park.

travellers, the pub claims to be the oldest in the Territory (its liquor licence has been valid since 1893).

The Drive ›› Point the car north along the Stuart Hwy and 160km later you'll arrive in Mataranka. En route, watch for tiny Larrimah, where the quirky and cheerfully rustic Pink Panther (Larrimah) Hotel serves camel or buffalo pies as well as Devonshire teas – go figure. By Mataranka, you're well and truly in the tropics.

TRIP HIGHLIGHT

7 Katherine (p71)

Katherine is probably best known for the Nitmiluk (Katherine Gorge) National Park to the east, and the town makes an obvious base, with plenty of accommodation and good opportunities to immerse yourself in the picturesque surroundings and local Indigenous culture. By day, spend your time exploring the burgeoning world of Aboriginal art at **Top Didj Cultural Experience & Art Gallery** (☎08-8971 2751; www.topdidj.com; cnr Gorge & Jaensch Rds; cultural experience adult/child/family $65/45/200; ⏲cultural experience 9.30am & 2.30pm Sun-Fri, 9.30am & 1.30pm Sat), a good place to see Aboriginal artists at work, the stunning new **Godinymayin Yijard Rivers Arts & Culture Centre** (☎08-8972 3751; www.gyracc.org.au; Stuart Hwy, Katherine East; ⏲10am-5pm Tue-Fri, to 3pm Sat), and Aboriginal-owned **Djilpin Arts** (☎08-8971 1770; www.djilpinarts.org.au; 27 Katherine Tce; ⏲9am-4pm Mon-Fri). As the sun nears the horizon, change pace entirely by joining the evening croc-spotting cruise of **Crocodile Night Adventure** (☎1800 089 103; www.travelnorth.com.au; adult/child $75/49; ⏲6.30pm May-Oct).

The Drive ›› There's not long to go now, at least by outback standards. On the final, steamy 314km into Darwin, name check the tiny settlements of Pine Creek and Adelaide River, before the clamour of wall-to-wall settlements on the Darwin approach will have you longing for the eternal outback horizon.

8 Darwin (p75)

Australia's only tropical capital city, Darwin gazes out confidently across the Timor Sea. It's closer to Bali than Bondi and can certainly feel far removed from the rest of the country.

Rainbow bee eaters, Darwin

Alice Springs to Adelaide

Alice to Adelaide connects two radically different Aussie belles, from the heart of the outback to the quiet sophistication of the south, along a suitably epic trail.

TRIP HIGHLIGHTS

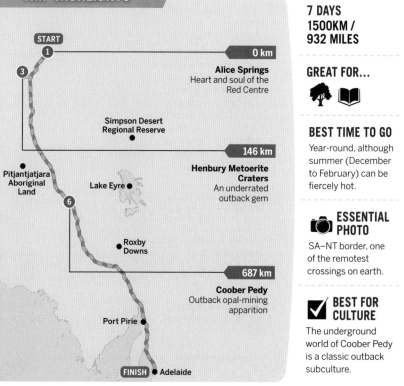

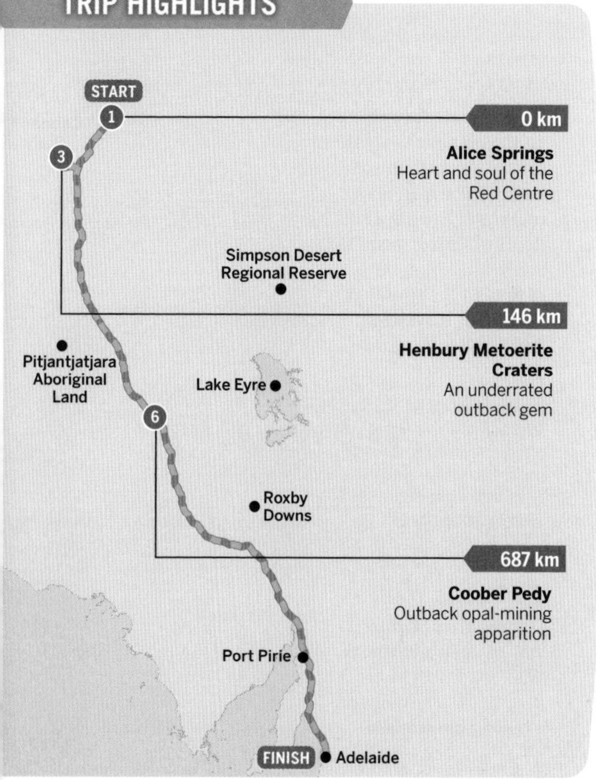

7 DAYS
1500KM / 932 MILES

GREAT FOR...

BEST TIME TO GO

Year-round, although summer (December to February) can be fiercely hot.

ESSENTIAL PHOTO

SA–NT border, one of the remotest crossings on earth.

BEST FOR CULTURE

The underground world of Coober Pedy is a classic outback subculture.

Left The Breakaways, Coober Pedy (p37)

3 Alice Springs to Adelaide

Set the GPS for the south and get on that road – you've a long drive ahead of you. Before you've gone too far, there are a couple of fine local Northern Territory landmarks to enjoy before the long, long road down through the South Australian heartland takes you to Coober Pedy and on to the coast.

TRIP HIGHLIGHT

❶ Alice Springs (p57)

There are many Alices to enjoy, from its role as a cultural capital of Aboriginal Australia to being a base for all that's good about Australia's Red Centre. Begin by taking in the tremendous view, particularly at sunrise and sunset, from the top of Anzac Hill, known as Untyeyetweleye in Arrernte; it's possible to walk (use Lions Walk from Wills Tce) or drive up. From the war memorial there's a 365-degree view over the town down to Heavitree Gap and the Ranges. Outback creatures found nowhere else on the planet are another central Australian speciality – learn all about reptiles at Alice Springs Reptile Centre, then visit everything from birds of prey to the speckled grunter at the Alice Springs Desert Park.

The Drive ›› The Stuart Hwy that cleaves the Northern Territory in two continues south of Alice; 91km down the road (which you'll share with the tour buses en route to Uluru) you'll come to Stuarts Well.

❷ Stuarts Well

Drivers are urged to 'have a spell' at Stuarts Well. It's worth stopping in for a burger and a beer at **Jim's Place**

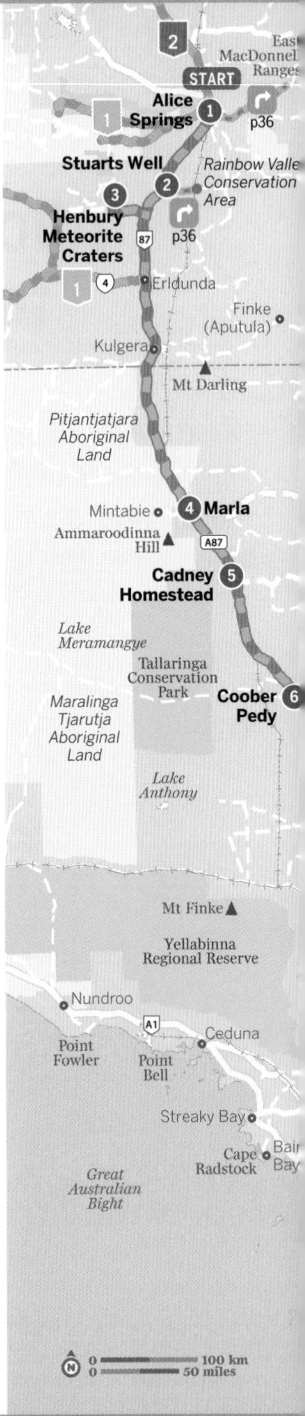

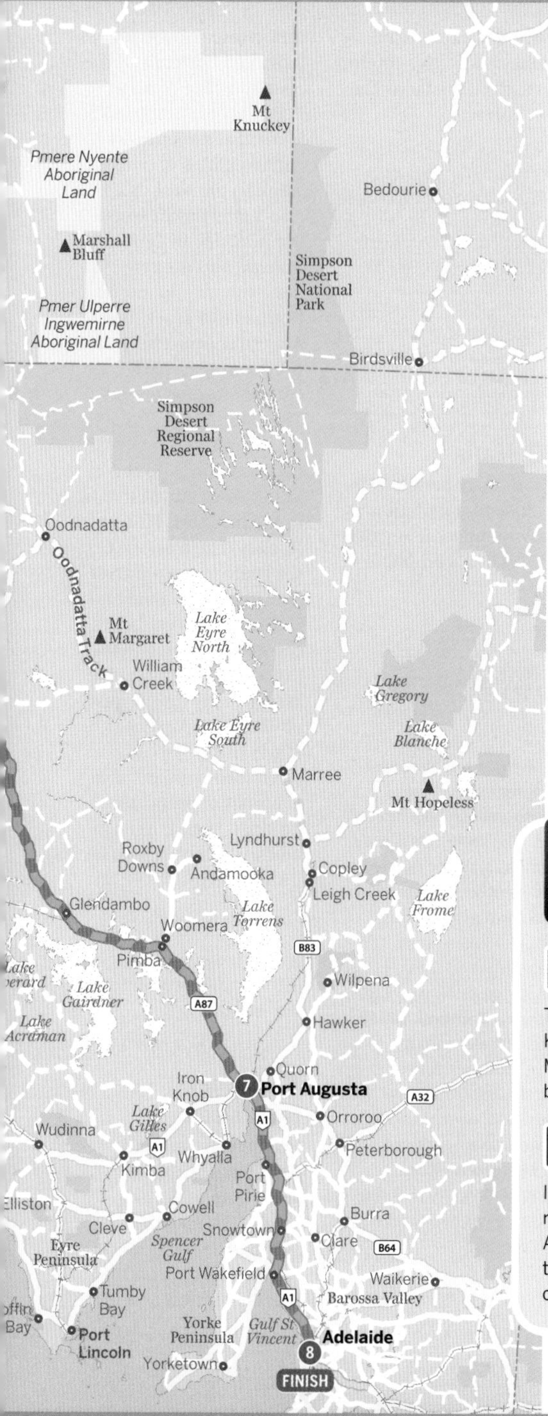

(☎08-8956 0808, 08-8952 2111; unpowered/powered sites $20/25, budget r with own swag/supplied linen $15/30, cabins s/d $75/95; ❄@🏊), run by well-known outback identity Jim Cotterill, who along with his father opened up Kings Canyon to tourism. You might also catch a performance by Dinky the singing and piano-playing dingo...

The Drive » Some 39km southwest of Stuarts Well, watch for the signs to the Henbury Meteorite Craters, 16km off the highway along an unsealed road that's fine for 2WDs if you proceed carefully.

TRIP HIGHLIGHT

❸ Henbury Meteorite Craters

In the rush to the big-ticket attractions of the Red Centre, this cluster of

LINK YOUR TRIP

1 Uluru & the Red Centre

This trip to Uluru, the Olgas, Kings Canyon and the West MacDonnell Ranges passes by Alice en route.

2 Alice Springs to Darwin

If you've done Trip 3 in reverse (ie from Adelaide to Alice), keep heading north to Darwin to cross the continent.

12 small craters, formed after a meteor fell to earth 4700 years ago, is well worth a detour. These are no mere potholes – the largest of the craters is 180m wide and 15m deep – and the crater floors are, in most cases, sprinkled lightly with green trees, giving the deeper of them a palpable sense of a lost, hidden oasis – they're invisible in some cases from a distance and only reveal themselves when you reach the crater rim. The surrounding country is wildly beautiful in an outback kind of way – red-hued earth, sand dunes and rocky outcrops extend out as far as the eye can see.

The Drive » Return 5km to the Ernest Giles Rd, a rough, 4WD-only back route to Kings Canyon, then 11km to the Stuart Hwy. Then it's 162km to the border, with a further 160km into Marla on the South Australian side. The last fuel before Marla is at Kulgera, 20km north of the border and 200km short of Marla.

❹ Marla

Marla may be small (its transient population usually numbers fewer than 250) but it's an important service centre for long-haul drivers and the peoples of the Anangu Pitjantjatjara traditional lands that sweep away in endless plains of mulga scrub to the west. It's also a stop on the Ghan, the Adelaide-to-Darwin railway, and it's here that the legendary, lonesome Oodnadatta Track, one of Australia's most famous 4WD traverses of the outback, begins or ends. The Oodnadatta Track is an unsealed, 615km road between Marla on the Stuart Hwy and Marree in the northern Flinders Ranges. The track traces the route of the old Overland Telegraph Line and the defunct Great Northern Railway. Lake Eyre, the world's sixth-largest lake (usually dry), is just off the road. As such, Marla is a crossroads town whose importance is far out of proportion to its size – treat it as such and you're unlikely to be disappointed.

The Drive » Beyond Marla, the pancake-flat Stuart Hwy goes to Cadney Homestead (82km) and all the way into Coober Pedy.

❺ Cadney Homestead

Out here in the South Australian outback, small landmarks and lonely settlements take on singular importance, both in warding off the great emptiness and in

DETOUR: EAST MACDONNELL RANGES & RAINBOW VALLEY

Start: ❶ Alice Springs

Although overshadowed by the more popular West Macs, the **East MacDonnell Ranges** are no less picturesque and, with fewer visitors, can be a more enjoyable outback experience. The sealed Ross Hwy runs 100km east of Alice Springs along the ranges, which are intersected by a series of scenic gaps and gorges. The gold-mining ghost town of Arltunga is 33km off the Ross Hwy along an unsealed road that is usually OK for 2WD vehicles.

Even better, south of Alice Springs, 24km off the Stuart Hwy along a 4WD track, the **Rainbow Valley Conservation Area** is a series of freestanding sandstone bluffs and cliffs, in shades ranging from cream to red. It's one of central Australia's more extraordinary sights. A marked walking trail takes you past claypans and in between the multihued outcrops to the aptly named **Mushroom Rock**. Rainbow Valley is most striking in the early morning or at sunset, but the area's silence will overwhelm you whatever time of day you are here.

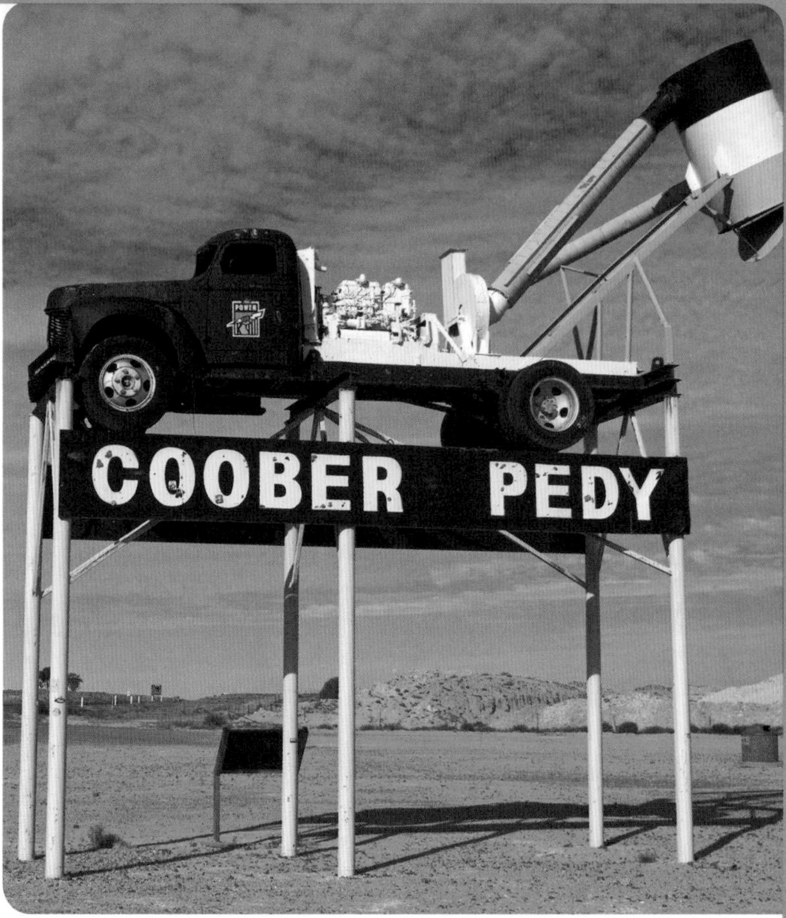

KRZYSZTOF DYDYNSKI/GETTY IMAGES ©

Mining blower truck at the entrance to Coober Pedy

orientating and servicing the needs of travellers. **Cadney Homestead** (☎08-8670 7994; cadney@bigpond.com; Stuart Hwy; unpowered/powered sites from $16/25, d cabin/motel $85/125; ❄@≋), 82km southeast of Marla, is one such place with caravan and tent sites, serviceable motel rooms and basic cabins (BYO towel to use the shared caravan park facilities), plus petrol, puncture repairs, takeaways, cold beer, an ATM, a swimming pool... Ask at the homestead about road conditions on the dirt track running west of the settlement – the track is usually passable in a 2WD vehicle, at least as far as the striking and rather aptly named **Painted Desert**. The track runs eventually to Oodnadatta.

The Drive » It's 152km from Cadney to Coober Pedy.

TRIP HIGHLIGHT

❻ Coober Pedy (p88)

As you pull into the world-famous opal-mining town of Coober Pedy, the dry, barren desert suddenly becomes riddled with holes, literally millions of them, and adjunct piles of dirt – quite suitably, the name derives from local Aboriginal words *kupa* (white man) and *piti* (hole). Check out the **Big Winch** (see p88), from which there are sweeping views over Coober Pedy. Take a tour with **Coober Pedy Tours** (☎08-8672 5223; www.cooberpedytours.com; 2hr tours adult/child from $50/25) and a scenic flight with **Opal Air** (☎08-8670 7997; www.opalair.com.au; flights per person from $470) to really take it all in.

The Drive » It's 540km from Coober Pedy to Port Augusta, and it still feels like the outback all the way, with horizonless plains and shimmering salt pans shadowing the road as far as Woomera (366km). Thereafter, the road tracks southeast for 174km into Port Augusta.

DIANA MAYFIELD/GETTY IMAGES ©

7 Port Augusta (p91)

Port Augusta proclaims itself to be the 'Crossroads of Australia' and it's not difficult to see why – highways and railways roll west across the Nullarbor into WA, north to the Flinders Ranges or Darwin, south to Adelaide or Port Lincoln, and east to Sydney. Given that you've just come in from the Never Never, there are two places that really speak to the spirit of the whole journey you're on. Just north of town, the excellent **Australian Arid Lands Botanic Garden** has 250 hectares of sand hills, clay flats and desert flora and fauna. Just as interesting is the **Wadlata Outback Centre**, a combined museum-visitor centre containing the 'Tunnel of Time', which traces local Aboriginal and European histories using audiovisual displays, interactive exhibits and a distressingly big snake.

The Drive » The final stretch from Port Augusta to Adelaide is the antithesis of where you've been so far – busy roadside towns at regular intervals, frequent glimpses of water, constant traffic and even a dual-carriage motorway for the last 95km into Adelaide.

Holy Cow Chai tent, WOMADelaide world music festival (p96), Adelaide

8 Adelaide (p92)

Sophisticated, cultured, neat-casual – this is the self-image Adelaide projects and in this it bears little resemblance to the frontier charms of the outback. For decades this 'City of Churches' had a slightly staid reputation, but these days things are different. Multicultural flavours infuse Adelaide's restaurants; there's a pumping arts and live-music scene; and the city's festival calendar has vanquished dull Saturday nights. There are still plenty of church spires here, but they're hopelessly outnumbered by pubs and a growing number of hip bars tucked away in lanes. You're also on the cusp of some of Australia's most celebrated wine regions, but that's a whole other story...

Outback New South Wales

4

From Bathurst to Broken Hill, this vast east–west New South Wales traverse takes you from the food-and-wine hinterland of Sydney to the profound silences and quirky towns of the outback.

TRIP HIGHLIGHTS

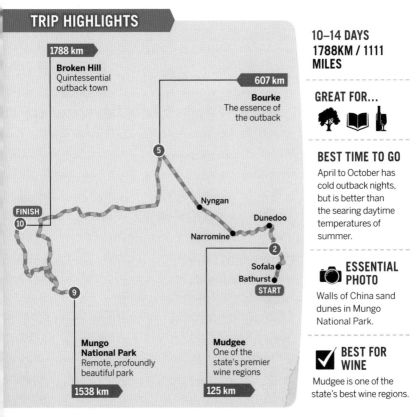

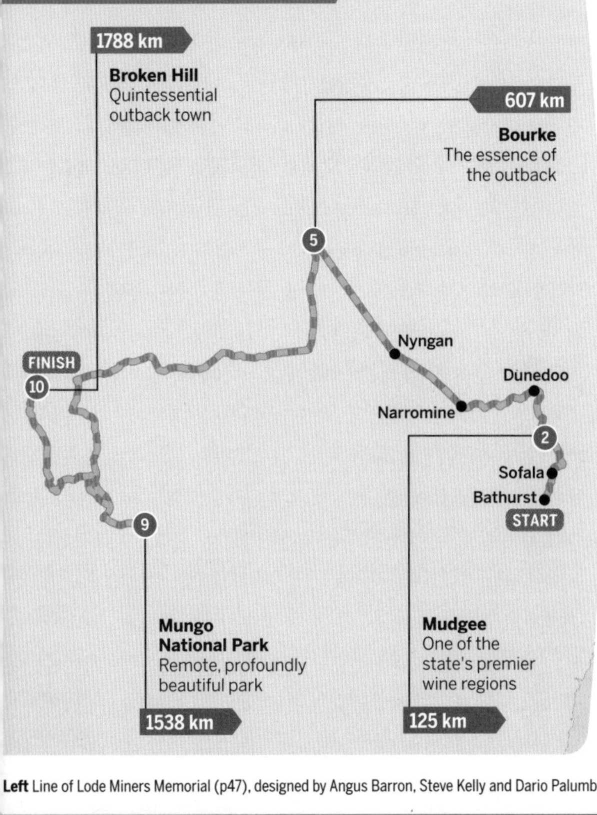

10–14 DAYS
1788KM / 1111 MILES

GREAT FOR...

BEST TIME TO GO

April to October has cold outback nights, but is better than the searing daytime temperatures of summer.

ESSENTIAL PHOTO

Walls of China sand dunes in Mungo National Park.

BEST FOR WINE

Mudgee is one of the state's best wine regions.

Left Line of Lode Miners Memorial (p47), designed by Angus Barron, Steve Kelly and Dario Palumbo

4 Outback New South Wales

You've heard about the outback. The only way to get there is via long and empty roads that pass through fascinating, isolated communities whose very names – Bourke, Wilcannia and Broken Hill – carry a whiff of outback legend. Before heading for the 'Back of Bourke', however, take time to sample the culinary and architectural treasures of civilisation in Bathurst, Mudgee and Gulgong.

1 Bathurst (p104)

Australia's oldest inland settlement, Bathurst has historical references strewn across its old centre, especially in the beautiful, manicured central square where formidable Victorian buildings transport you to the past; the most impressive of these is the 1880 **Courthouse** (p104), and don't miss the utterly fascinating **Australian Fossil & Mineral Museum** (www.somervillecollection.com.au; 224 Howick St; adult/child $12/6; ⏲10am-4pm Mon-Sat,

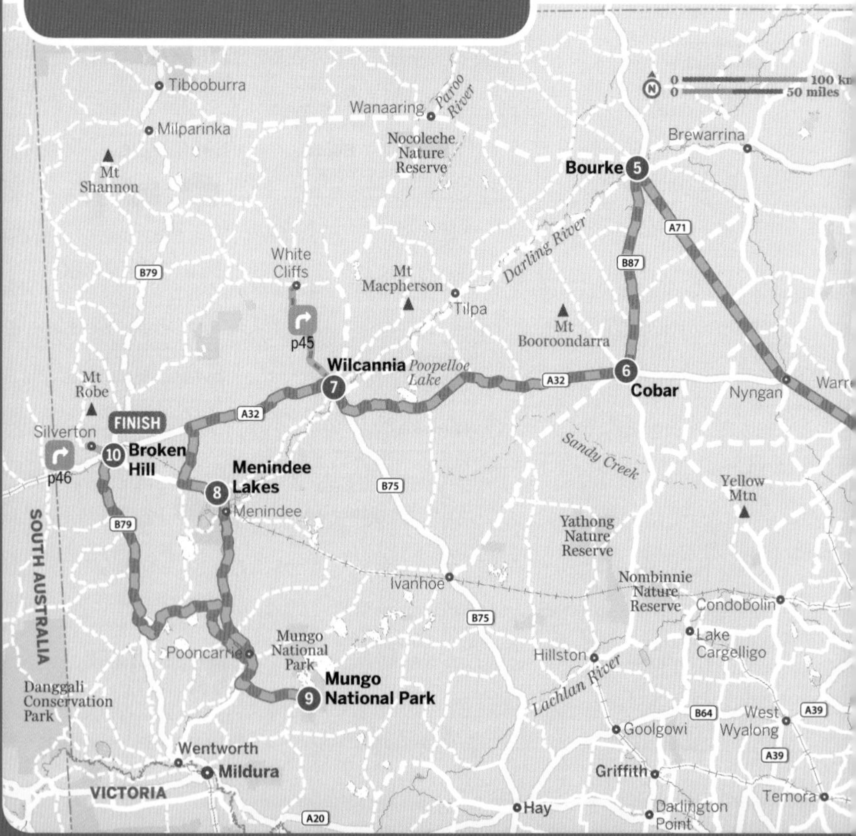

to 2pm Sun) complete with Australia's only complete skeleton of *Tyrannosaurus rex*. But this is no static open-air architectural museum. Instead, Bathurst displays a Sydney sensibility when it comes to enjoying good food and wines. And then, in a dramatic change of pace, it's also the bastion of Australian motorsports: if you're a devotee of motorsports, head to the **Mt Panorama Motor Racing Circuit** (www.mount-panorama.com.au), home to the epic Bathurst 1000 V8 race each October, as well as the **National Motor Racing Museum** (www.nmrm.com.au; Murrays Corner, Mt Panorama; adult/child $12.50/5.50; ⏲9am-4.30pm).

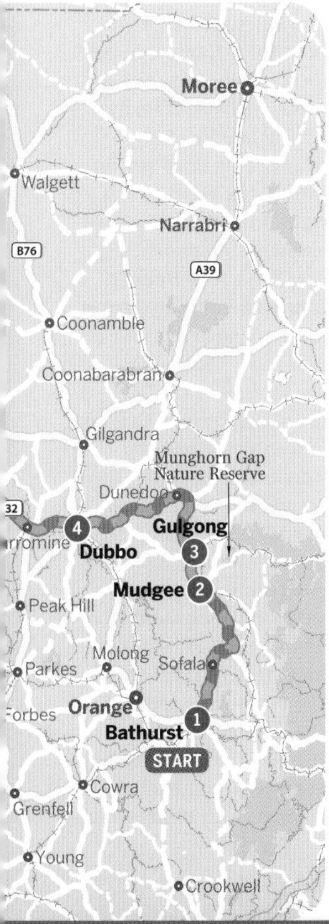

The Drive » Follow the signs towards Lithgow from Bathurst city centre, then take the turn-off for Sofala, before joining the main road to Mudgee (209km from Bathurst).

TRIP HIGHLIGHT

❷ Mudgee (p105)

The name Mudgee is an Aboriginal word for 'nest in the hills', a fitting name for this pretty town surrounded by vineyards and rolling hills. The wineries come hand-in-hand with excellent food, making Mudgee a popular weekend getaway (which is why we recommend visiting during the week). Mudgee's 35 cellar doors (all family-owned operations) are primarily clustered northeast of town – check out www.mudgeewine.com.au for further details. If wine's why you're here, consider taking a guided excursion with **Mudgee Wine & Country Tours** (☎02-6372 2367; www.mudgeewinetours.com.au; half-/full-day wine tours $50/80) or **Mudgee Tourist Bus** (☎02-6372 4475; www.mudgeetouristbus.com.au; half-/full-day wine tours $45/70), stop by Mudgee's best (and NSW's oldest) wine bar, **Roth's** (www.rothswinebar.com.au; 30 Market St; ⏲5pm-midnight Wed-Sat), and consider dropping everything to be here in September for the three-week **Mudgee Wine & Food Festival** (www.mudgeewine.com.au). And if you're visiting the wineries under your own steam, begin with **Lowe Wines** (☎03-6372 0800; www.lowewine.com.au; Tinja Lane; ⏲10am-5pm) and **Robert Stein Winery & Vineyard** (www.robertstein.com.au; Pipeclay Lane; ⏲10am-4.30pm).

The Drive » On the main Ulan Rd, around 29km after leaving Mudgee, follow the signs for Gulgong, which lies 24km away through dense, fire-scarred forest.

❸ Gulgong

To catch a glimpse of a small, rural, timbered Australian country town as it once was, there's nowhere better than Gulgong. And it's not just we who think so – this sweet, time-warped town once featured alongside author Henry Lawson on the $10 note. Australia's most famous poet, Lawson spent part of his childhood in Gulgong and, suitably, the town celebrates a **Henry Lawson Heritage Festival** during the June long weekend, with concerts at the Opera House and other festivities, and there's the **Henry Lawson Centre** (www.henrylawsongulgong.org.au; 147 Mayne St; adult/child $6/4; ⏲10am-3.30pm Mon-Sat, to 1pm Sun), which explores his life and works, as well

SCENIC ROUTES: BATHURST TO MUDGEE

The region north of Bathurst is good driving territory with beautiful scenery, parks and reserves and a handful of quaint little towns. An easy drive through increasingly rolling country dips down into a valley 43km northeast of Bathurst. Just before crossing the bridge, detour along the charming, ramshackle main street of **Sofala**, a pretty hangover from the region's gold-mining days – it's such a perfect evocation of a semi-abandoned mining village that you'll wonder whether it's custom made. From Sofala continue for 28km to Ilford, where you join the main Lithgow–Mudgee road. As you head northwest, you'll pass pretty Lake Windamere before reaching Mudgee. Ignore the town's untidy outskirts and head for the centre, taking Church St which becomes Ulan Rd, which in turn heads northwest of town past some of the best wineries. Some 11km out of Mudgee, consider a detour to the **Munghorn Gap Nature Reserve**, where there's the popular 8km-return Castle Rock walking trail; the reserve is home to the endangered regent's honeyeater.

as his early memories of the town. Today the narrow, rambling streets, classified by the National Trust, are not so done-up that they have lost their charm: we recommend a gentle wander up and down the main street to really see what we mean.

The Drive » From Gulgong, loop north along Rte 86 and pass through Birriwa before turning left (west) at Dunedoo. From there, it's 87 dry and dusty kilometres into Dubbo.

4 Dubbo (p106)

It's at Dubbo that you get the first hint of what lies ahead – there's a dryness in the air in this big-sky country and to the west of here the outback really begins. With that in mind, Dubbo takes on the appearance of the last big city before the desert (and eternity) begins. Before venturing out in the void, there are three attractions that seem perfectly suited to this vast and barren land. With unfailingly clear skies to encourage you, **Dubbo Observatory** is a place to stargaze; advance bookings are essential. Then there's a glimpse of the wild at **Taronga Western Plains Zoo** (p106), one of the best zoos in regional Australia. And finally, there's **Dundullimal**, about 2km beyond the zoo, a National Trust timber-slab homestead built in the 1840s and an exemplary example of the remote and rural homestead of Australian lore.

The Drive » It's time to fill your tank with petrol and head for the outback. And the directions here are simple: take the Mitchell Hwy and stay on it all the way to Bourke (369km) via Narromine. It's dry country out here: the sand turns from yellow to orange and the foliage turns to scrub. Welcome to the outback fringe.

TRIP HIGHLIGHT

5 Bourke (p107)

Australian poet Henry Lawson once said, 'If you know Bourke, you know Australia.' Immortalised for Australians in the expression 'back of Bourke' (in the middle of nowhere), this town sits on the edge of the outback, miles from anywhere and sprawled along the Darling River. The **Back O' Bourke Exhibition Centre** is an excellent exhibition space that follows the legends of the back country (both Indigenous and settler) through interactive displays – ask about its packages that include a river cruise on the PV *Jandra*, an entertaining outback show, and a bus tour of the town and surrounds (note that the cruise and show operate April to October only). And then there's Bourke's **historic cemetery**, peppered with epitaphs like 'perished in the bush'; Professor Fred Hollows, the renowned eye surgeon, is buried here. If you're keen to explore on your own, ask for the leaflet called *Back O'Bourke Mud Map Tours.*

The Drive » Rte 87, lined with dull eucalyptus greens and scrubby horizons, runs due south of Bourke for 160km with not a single town to speak of en route.

6 Cobar

Out here, a town doesn't need to have much to have you dreaming of arriving. It might be just a petrol station, but occasionally a place has a little more to detain you. And on this score, Cobar fits the bill perfectly. It's a bustling mining town with a productive copper mine, and as something of a regional centre down through the decades, it even boasts a handful of interesting buildings – true to old colonial form, these include the **old courthouse** and **cop station**. And even if you're not the museum type, don't miss the **Cobar Museum** (adult/child/family $8/6/18; ⌚8.30am-5pm) at the Great Cobar Heritage Centre: it has sophisticated displays on the environment, local Aboriginal life and the early Europeans. Watch also for the Big Beer Can, Cobar's contribution to that strange provincial Australian need to erect oversized and decidedly kitsch monuments to the prosaic icons of Aussie life.

The Drive » It's not quite the Nullarbor (Australia's straightest road), but the Barrier Hwy is very long and very straight, all 250km of it into Wilcannia. Long straw-coloured paddocks line the roadside until, all of a sudden, you're crossing the Darling River and its tree-lined riverbanks at the entrance to town.

7 Wilcannia (p108)

In the old times, Wilcannia was one of the great river ports of inland Australia, and it still boasts a fine collection of old sandstone buildings dating from this prosperous heyday in the 1880s. In more recent times, the town and its large Indigenous population have become a poster child for Aboriginal disadvantage and hopelessness. With this modern history in mind, it should come as no surprise that Wilcannia (www.wilcanniatourism.com.au) hasn't in the recent past had a lot of love from travellers. But it can be a fascinating, complicated place where the certainties and optimism of modern Australia seem a whole lot less clear. Make of it what you will.

DETOUR: WHITE CLIFFS

Start: 7 Wilcannia

There are few stranger places in Australia than the tiny pock-marked opal-mining town of White Cliffs (www.whitecliffsnsw.com.au), 93km northwest of Wilcannia along the sealed Opal Miners Way. Surrounded by pretty hostile country and enduring temperatures that soar well past 40°C in summer, many residents have moved underground, Coober Pedy–style, to escape the heat. You can visit opal showrooms where local miners sell their finds (these are well signed), or try fossicking around the old diggings, where you'll see interpretative signs. Watch your step as many of the shafts are open and unsigned. If you can't face the long haul back to civilisation, you can stay underground at the **White Cliffs Underground Motel** (☎08-8091 6677; www.undergroundmotel.com.au; s/d with shared bathroom incl breakfast $115/145;) – custom-built with a tunnelling machine. It has a pool, a lively dining room and simple, cool, silent rooms. The motel's museum on local life is very good – it's free for guests, but a pricey $10 for nonguests.

The Drive » Dusty backcountry trails head southwest from Wilcannia, but continue southwest along the Barrier Hwy for 119km, then take one such trail south off the main highway towards Menindee Lakes. Along the 52 unpaved kilometres (fine for 2WD vehicles) you'll pass remote homesteads before turning left on the MR66 for the final 48km into Menindee.

8 Menindee Lakes

Out here, water can seem like a vision of paradise, and Menindee Lakes, which fan out from the scruffy town of Menindee, are no exception. This series of nine natural, ephemeral lakes adjacent to the Darling River are rich in bird life, and the dead trees in the shallows make for some photogenic corners. If you've planned ahead, bring a picnic, visit the **visitor centre** (☎08-8091 4274; www.menindeelakes.com; Yartla St) in Menindee town for a map, and head out to soak up the miracle of water in the epic, otherwise empty land.

The Drive » Unless it has been raining, which is rare out here, take the unsealed gravel-and-sand road that heads south from Menindee for around 120km, then follow the signs east for 41km into Mungo National Park. This is dry, barren country, deliciously remote and filled with sparse desert flora and fauna.

TRIP HIGHLIGHT

9 Mungo National Park (p108)

One of Australia's most soulful places, this isolated, beautiful and important park covers 278.5 sq km of the Willandra Lakes Region World Heritage Area. It is one of Australia's most accessible slices of the true outback, where big red kangaroos and emus graze the plains and unimpeded winds shape the land into the strangest shapes. Lake Mungo is a dry lake and site of the oldest archaeological finds in Australia, as

DETOUR: SILVERTON

Start: 10 Broken Hill

If you think Broken Hill is remote, try visiting quirky Silverton (www.silverton.org.au), an old silver-mining town and now an almost-ghost town. Visiting is like walking into a Russell Drysdale painting. Silverton's fortunes peaked in 1885, when it had a population of 3000, but in 1889 the mines closed and the people (and some houses) moved to Broken Hill. It stirs into life every now and then – Silverton was the setting for films such as *Mad Max II* and *A Town Like Alice*. The town's heart and soul is the **Silverton Hotel** (☎08-8088 5313; Layard St; ⏲9am-11pm), which displays film memorabilia and walls covered with miscellany typifying Australia's peculiar brand of larrikin humour. The 1889 **Silverton Gaol** (adult/child $4/1; ⏲9.30am-4pm) once housed 14 cells; today the museum is a treasure trove: room after room is crammed full of a century of local life (wedding dresses, typewriters, mining equipment, photos). The **School Museum** (adult/child $2.50/1; ⏲9.30am-3.30pm Mon, Wed, Fri-Sun) is another history pit stop, tracing the local school from its earliest incarnation in a tent in 1884. Considerably more offbeat is the **Mad Max 2 Museum** (Stirling St; adult/child $7.50/5; ⏲10am-4pm), the culmination of Englishman Adrian Bennett's lifetime obsession with the theme.

To get here, take the A32 out of town (direction Adelaide). Almost immediately, the Silverton road branches off to the northwest – it's 25km from Broken Hill to Silverton. The road beyond Silverton becomes isolated and the horizons vast, but it's worth driving 5km to **Mundi Mundi Lookout** where the view over the plain is so extensive it reveals the curvature of the Earth.

JULIE FLETCHER/GETTY IMAGES ©

Menindee Lakes

well as being the longest continual record of Aboriginal life (the world's oldest recorded cremation site has been found here), dating back more than 50,000 years, making the history of European settlement on this continent seem like the mere blink of an eye. The undoubted highlight here, aside from the blissful sense of utter remoteness, is the fabulous 33km semicircle ('lunette') of sand dunes known as **Walls of China**, created by the unceasing westerly wind. From the visitor centre a road leads across the dry lake bed to a car park, then it's a short walk to the viewing platform. For more information on the park, visit www.visitmungo.com.au.

The Drive » Numerous trails lead to Broken Hill, and none of them are paved (but nor do they require a 4WD unless the rains have been heavy). Return north to Menindee (from where it's 118 paved kilometres into Broken Hill), or cross the skein of tracks west to the paved Silver City Hwy which also leads to Broken Hill.

TRIP HIGHLIGHT

⑩ Broken Hill (p110)

The massive silver skimp dump that forms a backdrop for Broken Hill's town centre accentuates the unique character of this desert frontier town somewhere close to the end of the earth.

One of the most memorable experiences of Broken Hill is viewing the sunset from the **Sculpture Symposium** (Nine Mile Rd; admission to reserve adult/child $5/2) on the highest hilltop 12km from town. The sculptures are the work of 12 international artists who carved the huge sandstone blocks on-site. Other highlights include: the **Palace Hotel** (☎08-8088 1699; www.thepalacehotelbrokenhill.com.au; cnr Argent & Sulphide Sts), the astonishing star of the hit Australian movie *The Adventures of Priscilla, Queen of the Desert*; the **Line of Lode Miners Memorial** (Federation Way; ⏰6am-9pm), with its poignant stories and memorable views; the **Pro Hart Gallery** (www.prohart.com.au; 108 Wyman St; adult/child $5/3; ⏰10am-5pm Mar-Nov, to 4pm Dec-Feb); and the **Royal Flying Doctor Service** (☎08-8080 3714; www.flyingdoctor.org.au/Broken-Hill-Base.html; Airport Rd; adult/child $8.50/4; ⏰9am-5pm Mon-Fri, 10am-3pm Sat & Sun).

Destinations

Uluru, Alice & the Red Centre (p50)

Visit stunning Uluru and Kata Tjuta, or explore the awesome gorge of Kings Canyon in Watarrka National Park.

North to Darwin (p70)

From the deserts to the tropics, the Northern Territory is a splendid place to be during Australia's winter months.

South to Adelaide (p88)

The road south will take you through Coober Pedy, where opal-crazed locals beat the desert heat in 'cool' underground houses.

Outback New South Wales (p104)

Explore this remote pocket of New South Wales, full of sleepy towns and dazzling displays of nature.

Ormiston Gorge, West MacDonnell Ranges (p68)

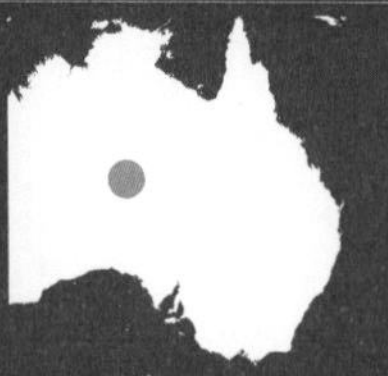

Uluru, Alice & the Red Centre

The Red Centre is Australia's heartland, boasting the iconic attractions of Uluru and Kata Tjuta, plus an enigmatic central desert culture that continues to produce extraordinary abstract art.

ULURU (AYERS ROCK)

The first sight of Uluru on the horizon will astound even the most jaded traveller. Uluru is 3.6km long and rises a towering 348m from the surrounding sandy scrubland (867m above sea level). If that's not impressive enough, it's believed that two-thirds of the rock lies beneath the sand. Closer inspection reveals a wondrous contoured surface concealing numerous sacred sites of particular significance to the Anangu. If your first sight of Uluru is during the afternoon, it appears as an ochre-brown colour, scored and pitted by dark shadows. As the sun sets, it illuminates the rock in burnished orange, then a series of deeper reds before it fades into charcoal. A performance in reverse, with marginally fewer spectators, is given at dawn.

Activities

There are walking tracks around Uluru, and ranger-led walks explain the area's plants, wildlife, geology and cultural significance. All the trails are flat and suitable for wheelchairs. Several areas of spiritual significance are off limits to visitors; these are marked with fences and signs. The Anangu ask you not to photograph these sites.

The excellent *Visitor Guide & Maps* brochure, which can be picked up at the Cultural Centre, gives details on a few self-guided walks.

Base Walk WALKING

This track (10.6km, three to four hours) circumnavigates the rock, passing caves, paintings, sandstone folds and geological abrasions along the way.

Liru Walk WALKING

Links the Cultural Centre with the start of the Mala Walk and climb, and winds through strands of mulga before opening up near Uluru (4km return, 1½ hours).

Mala Walk WALKING

From the base of the climbing point (2km return, one hour), interpretive signs explain the *tjukurpa* (Aboriginal law, religion and custom) of the Mala (hare-wallaby people), which is significant to the Anangu, as well as fine examples of rock art. A ranger-guided walk (free) along this route departs at 10am (8am from October to April) from the car park.

Kuniya Walk WALKING

A short walk (1km return, 45 minutes) from the car park on the southern side leads to the most permanent waterhole, Mutitjulu, home of the ancestral watersnake. Great birdwatching and some excellent rock art are highlights of this walk.

Uluru Climb WALKING

The Anangu ask that visitors respect Aboriginal law by not climbing Uluru. The steep and demanding path (1.6km return, two hours) follows the traditional route taken by ancestral Mala men. The climb is often closed (sometimes at short notice) due to weather and Anangu business.

Sunset & Sunrise Viewing Areas

About halfway between Yulara and Uluru, the **sunset viewing area** has plenty of car and coach parking for that familiar postcard view. The **Talnguru Nyakunytjaku sunrise viewing area** is perched on a sand dune and captures both the Rock and Kata Tjuta (the Olgas) in all their glory. It also has two great interpretive walks (1.5km) about women's and men's business. There's a shaded viewing area, toilets and a place to picnic.

Yulara (Ayers Rock Resort)

POP 887

Yulara is the service village for the Uluru-Kata Tjuta National Park, and has effectively turned one of the world's least hospitable regions into a comfortable place to stay. Lying just outside the national park, 20km from Uluru and 53km from Kata Tjuta, the complex is the closest base for exploring the park.

Sights & Activities

The Ayers Rock Resort conducts numerous free activities throughout the day: from spear, boomerang and didgeridoo classes to dance programs. Pick up a program at your accommodation.

Sleeping

All of the accommodation in Yulara, including the camping ground and hostel, is owned by the Ayers Rock Resort. Even though there are almost 5000 beds, it's wise to make a reservation, especially during school holidays. Substantial discounts are usually offered if you book for more than two or three nights.

Ayers Rock Resort Campground CAMPGROUND $
(08-8957 7001; www.ayersrockresort.com.au/arrcamp; unpowered/powered sites $38/48, cabins $165;) A saviour for the budget conscious, this sprawling campground is set among native gardens. There are good facilities including a kiosk, free BBQs, a camp kitchen and a pool. During the peak season it's very busy, and the inevitable predawn convoy heading for Uluru can provide an unwanted wake-up call. The cramped cabins (shared facilities) sleep six people and are only really suitable for a family.

Uluru (Ayers Rock)

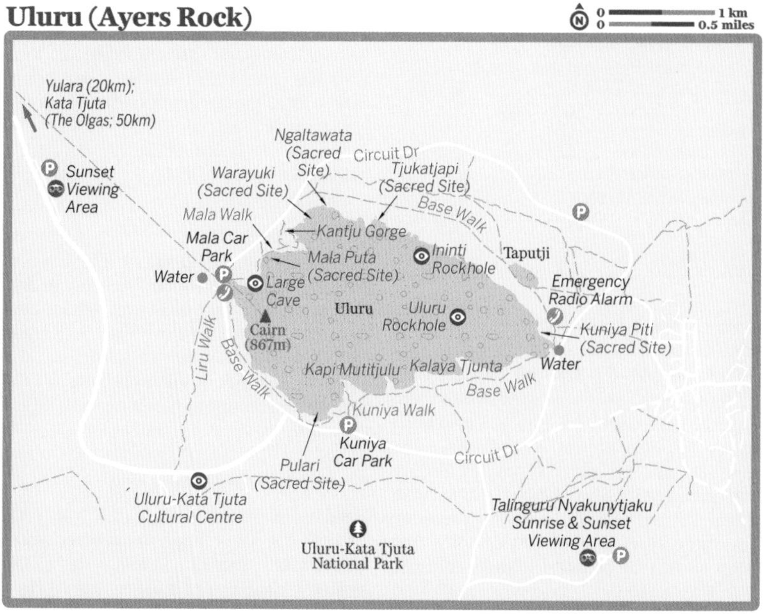

Yulara (Ayers Rock Resort)

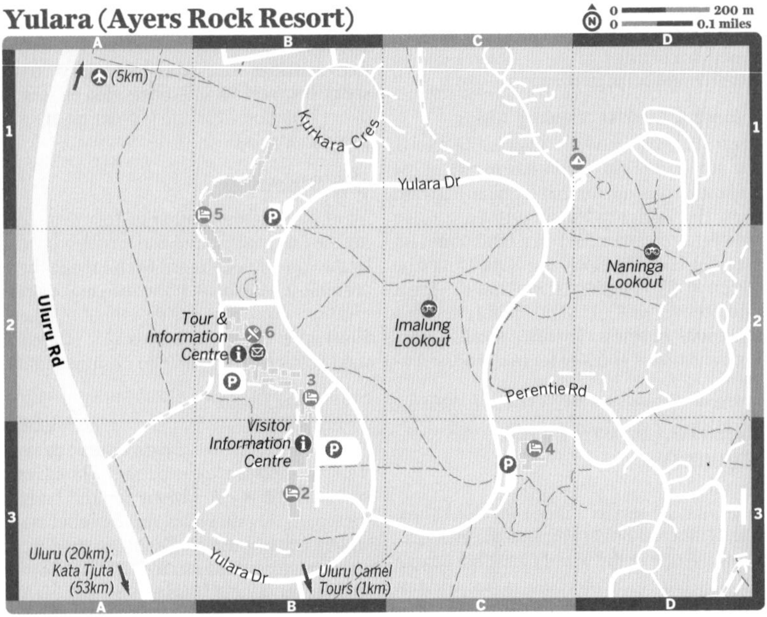

Outback Pioneer Hotel & Lodge HOSTEL $
(☎1300 134 044; www.ayersrockresort.com.au/outback; dm $38-46, d $240-310; ❄@🏊) With a lively bar, barbecue restaurant and musical entertainment, this is the budget choice for noncampers. The cheapest options are the 20-bed YHA unisex dorms, and squashy four-bed budget cabins with fridge, TV and shared bathroom. There are also more spacious motel-style rooms that sleep up to four people. Children under 12 stay free, though anyone over 12 is an extra $50 a night.

Emu Walk Apartments APARTMENTS $$$
(☎1300 134 044; www.ayersrockresort.com.au/emu; 1-/2-bedroom apt from $400/500; ❄🏊) The pick of the bunch for families looking for self-contained accommodation, Emu Walk has comfortable, modern apartments, each with a lounge room (with TV) and a well-equipped kitchen with washer and dryer. The one-bedroom apartments accommodate four people, while the two-bedroom version sleeps six.

Desert Gardens Hotel HOTEL $$$
(☎1300 134 044; r $410-530; ❄@🏊) One of Yulara's original hotels, and showing its age. This place gets very busy over school holiday periods, which can overwhelm cleaning staff, but generally service is friendly and efficient. The spacious deluxe rooms are the best option, featuring balconies with desert or Uluru views. A big buffet breakfast is served in the restaurant and there's a pleasant pool area shaded with gums.

Sails in the Desert HOTEL $$$
(☎1300 134 044; http://www.ayersrockresort.com.au/sails; superior d $540, ste $1000; ❄@📶🏊) The rooms still seem overpriced

at the resort's flagship hotel. There's a lovely pool and surrounding lawn shaded by sails and trees. There are also tennis courts, a health spa, several restaurants and a piano bar. The best rooms have balcony views of the rock – request one when you make a booking.

Eating

Walpa Lobby Bar MODERN AUSTRALIAN $$
(Sails in the Desert; mains $30; 11am-10pm) If you want to treat yourself, this is the place to try. With a recent makeover, and the feel of a Hilton Hotel bar, the excellent food and friendly service make up for the slight sterility. Hot and cold seafood platters are a treat, and most dishes feature Australian bush ingredients. Salads and antipasto also available. 'Walpa' is the Pitjantjatjara name for wind.

Geckos Cafe MEDITERRANEAN $$
(Resort Shopping Centre; mains $20-30; 11am-9pm;) For great value, a warm atmosphere and tasty food head to this buzzing licensed cafe. The wood-fired pizzas, pastas, burgers and fish and chips go well with a carafe of sangria, and the courtyard tables are a great place to enjoy the desert night air. There are several veggie and gluten-free options, plus meals can be made to takeaway.

Outback Pioneer Barbecue BARBECUE $$
(Outback Pioneer Hotel & Lodge; burgers $18, meat $30, salad bar only $17; 6-9pm) For a fun, casual night out, this lively tavern is the popular choice for everyone from backpackers to grey nomads. Choose between kangaroo skewers, prawns, veggie burgers, steaks and emu sausages, and grill them yourself at the communal BBQs. The deal includes a salad bar. In the same complex is the **Pioneer Kitchen** (Outback Pioneer Hotel & Lodge; meals $10-22; 6-9pm), doing brisk business in burgers, pizza and kiddie meals.

★ **Bough House** AUSTRALIAN $$$
(Outback Pioneer Hotel & Lodge; mains $30-40; 6.30-10am & 6.30-9.30pm;) This family-friendly, country-style place overlooks the pool at the Outback Pioneer. Intimate candlelit dining is strangely set in a barnlike dining room. Bough House specialises in native ingredients such as lemon myrtle, kakadu plums and bush tomatoes. Try the native tasting plate for a selection of Australian wildlife meats, and follow up with the braised wallaby shank for your main. The dessert buffet is free with your main course.

A QUESTION OF CLIMBING

Many visitors consider climbing Uluru to be a highlight of a trip to the Centre, and even a rite of passage. But for the traditional owners, the Anangu, Uluru is a sacred place. The path up the side of the Rock is part of the route taken by the Mala ancestors on their arrival at Uluru and has great spiritual significance – and is not to be trampled by human feet. When you arrive at Uluru you'll see a sign from the Anangu saying 'We don't climb', and a request that you don't climb either.

The Anangu are the custodians of Uluru and take responsibility for the safety of visitors. Any injuries or deaths that occur are a source of distress and sadness to them. For similar reasons of public safety, Parks Australia would prefer that people didn't climb. It's a very steep ascent, not to be taken lightly, and each year there are several air rescues, mostly of people suffering heart attacks. Furthermore, Parks Australia must constantly monitor the climb and close it on days where the temperature is forecast to reach 36°C or over, and when strong winds are expected.

So if the Anangu and Parks Australia don't want people to climb Uluru, why does the climb remain open? The answer is tourism. The tourism industry believes visitor numbers would drop significantly – at least initially – if the climb was closed, particularly among those who think there is nothing else to do at Uluru.

A commitment has been made to close the climb for good, but only when there are adequate new visitor experiences in place or when the proportion of visitors climbing falls below 20%. Until then, it remains a personal decision and a question of respect. Before deciding, visit the **Cultural Centre** (p55) and perhaps take an **Anangu guided tour** (p55).

Information

ANZ bank (☎ 08-8956 2070) Currency exchange and 24-hour ATMs.

Emergency (☎ ambulance 0420 101 403, police 08-8956 2166) For emergencies.

Internet Cafe (Outback Pioneer Hotel & Lodge; ⏲ 5am-11pm; 📶) In the backpacker common room.

Post Office (☎ 08-8956 2288; Resort Shopping Centre; ⏲ 9am-6pm Mon-Fri, 10am-2pm Sat & Sun) An agent for the Commonwealth and NAB banks. Pay phones are outside.

Royal Flying Doctor Service Medical Centre (☎ 08-8956 2286; ⏲ 9am-noon & 2-5pm Mon-Fri, 10-11am Sat & Sun) The resort's medical centre and ambulance service.

Tour & Information Centre (☎ 08-8957 7324; Resort Shopping Centre; ⏲ 8am-8pm) Most tour operators and car-hire firms have desks at this centre.

Visitor Information Centre (☎ 08-8957 7377; ⏲ 8.30am-4.30pm) Contains displays on the geography, wildlife and history of the region. There's a short audio tour ($2) if you want to learn more. It also sells books and regional maps.

Getting Around

A free shuttle bus meets all flights and drops off at all accommodation points around the resort; pick-up is 90 minutes before your flight. Another free shuttle bus loops through the resort – stopping at all accommodation points and the shopping centre – every 15 minutes from 10.30am to 6pm and from 6.30pm to 12.30am daily.

Uluru Express (☎ 08-8956 2152; www.uluru-express.com.au) falls somewhere between a shuttle-bus service and an organised tour. It provides return transport from the resort to Uluru and Kata Tjuta – see website for details.

Hiring a car will give you the flexibility to visit the Rock and the Olgas whenever you want. Car rental offices are at the Tour & Information Centre and Connellan Airport.

KATA TJUTA (THE OLGAS)

No journey to Uluru is complete without a visit to Kata Tjuta (the Olgas), a striking group of domed rocks huddled together about 35km west of the Rock. There are 36 boulders shoulder to shoulder forming deep valleys and steep-sided gorges. Many visitors find them even more captivating than their prominent neighbour. The tallest rock, **Mt Olga** (546m; 1066m above sea level) is approximately 200m higher than Uluru. Kata Tjuta means 'many heads' and is of great *tjukurpa* significance, particularly for men, so stick to the tracks.

The 7.4km **Valley of the Winds** loop (two to four hours) is one of the most challenging and rewarding bushwalks in the park. It winds through the gorges, giving excellent views of the surreal domes and traversing varied terrain. It's not particularly arduous, but wear sturdy shoes, and take plenty of water. Starting this walk at first light often rewards you with solitude, enabling you to appreciate the sounds of the wind and bird calls carried up the valley.

The short signposted track beneath towering rock walls into pretty **Walpa Gorge** (2.6km return, 45 minutes) is especially beautiful in the afternoon, when sunlight floods the gorge.

There's a picnic and sunset-viewing area with toilet facilities just off the access road a few kilometres west of the base of Kata Tjuta. Like Uluru, Kata Tjuta is at its glorious, blood-red best at sunset.

Uluru-Kata Tjuta National Park

There are some world-famous sights touted as unmissable, which end up being a letdown when you actually see them. And then there's Uluru: nothing can really prepare you for the immensity, grandeur, changing colour and stillness of 'the rock'. It really is a sight that will sear itself onto your mind.

The World Heritage-listed icon has attained the status of a pilgrimage. Uluru, the equally (some say more) impressive Kata Tjuta (the Olgas), and the surrounding area are of deep cultural significance to the traditional owners, the Pitjantjatjara and Yankuntjatjara Aboriginal peoples (who refer to themselves as Anangu). The Anangu officially own the national park, which is leased to Parks Australia and jointly administered.

There's plenty to see and do: meandering walks, bike rides, guided tours, desert culture and simply contemplating the many changing colours and moods of the great monolith itself.

The only accommodation is at the Ayers Rock Resort in the Yulara village, 20km from the Rock. Expect premium prices, reflecting the remote locale.

Information

The **park** (www.parksaustralia.gov.au/uluru/index.html; adult/child $25/free) is open from half an hour before sunrise to sunset daily (varying slightly between months – check the website for exact times). Entry permits are valid for three days and are available at the drive-through entry station on the road from Yulara.

Uluru-Kata Tjuta Cultural Centre (☎08-8956 1128; www.parksaustralia.gov.au/uluru/do/cultural-centre.html; ⏰7am-6pm) is 1km before Uluru on the road from Yulara and should be your first stop. Displays and exhibits focus on *tjukurpa* and the history and management of the national park. The information desk in the Nintiringkupai building is staffed by park rangers who supply the informative *Visitor Guide*, leaflets and walking notes.

The Cultural Centre encompasses the craft outlet **Maruku Arts** (☎08-8956 2558; www.maruku.com.au; ⏰8.30am-5.30pm), owned by about 20 Anangu communities from across central Australia (including the local Mutitjulu community), selling hand-crafted wooden carvings, bowls and boomerangs. **Walkatjara Art Centre** (☎08-8956 2537; ⏰9am-5.30pm) is a working art centre owned by the local Mutitjulu community. It focuses on paintings and ceramics created by women from Mutitjulu. **Ininti Cafe & Souvenirs** (☎08-8956 2214; ⏰7am-5pm) sells souvenirs such as T-shirts, ceramics, hats, CDs and a variety of books on Uluru, Aboriginal culture, bush foods and the flora and fauna of the area. The attached cafe serves ice cream, pies and light meals.

Tours

Seit Outback Australia BUS TOUR
(☎08-8956 3156; www.seitoutbackaustralia.com.au) This small group-tour operator has numerous options including a sunset tour around Uluru (adult/child $149/121), and a sunrise tour at Kata Tjuta for the same price and including breakfast and a walk into Walpa Gorge.

AAT Kings BUS TOUR
(☎08-8956 2171; www.aatkings.com) Operating the largest range of coach tours to Uluru, AAT offers a range of half- and full-day tours from Yulara. Check the website or enquire at the Tour & Information Centre (p54) in Yulara.

Uluru Camel Tours CAMEL TOUR
(☎08-8956 3333; www.ulurucameltours.com.au) View Uluru and Kata Tjuta from a distance atop a camel ($80, 1½ hours) or take the popular Camel to Sunrise and Sunset tours ($125, 2½ hours).

Kata Tjuta (The Olgas)

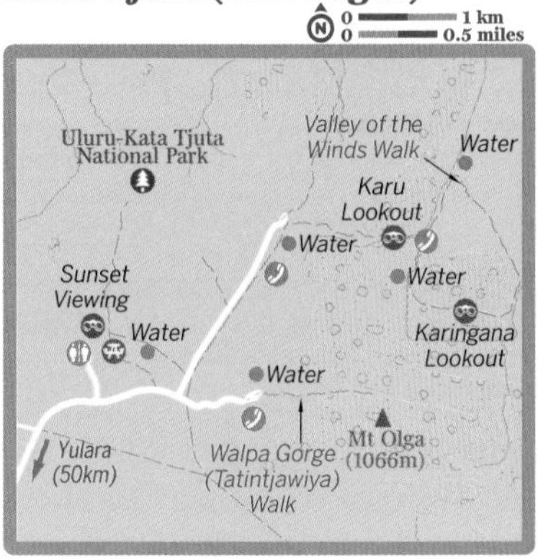

★ **Uluru Aboriginal Tours** CULTURAL TOUR
(☎0447 878 851; www.uluruaboriginaltours.com.au; guided tours from $99) Owned and operated by Anangu from the Mutitjulu community, this company offers a range of trips to give you an insight into the significance of the Rock through the eyes of the traditional owners. Tours operate and depart from the cultural centre (p55), as well as from Yulara Ayers Rock Resort (through AAT Kings) and from Alice Springs.

There are a range of tours, including the Rising Sun & Sacred Walk tour, which includes bush skills demonstrations, such as spear throwing, a hot buffet breakfast around a campfire, and unparalleled insights into the area's traditional lore and legend from your local guide. Call or email for the latest offerings of self-drive tours and packages.

Desert Tracks CULTURAL TOUR
(☎0439 500 419; www.deserttracks.com.au; adult/child $249/199) This Pitjantjatjara-run company offers a full-day 4WD journey into the remote Pitjantjatjara Lands to meet the traditional owners of Cave Hill and view some spectacular rock art depicting the Seven Sisters story.

Sounds of Silence DINING
(☎08-8957 7448; www.ayersrockresort.com.au/sounds-of-silence; adult/child $195/96) Waiters serve champagne and canapés on a desert dune with stunning sunset views of Uluru and Kata Tjuta. Then it's a buffet dinner (with emu, croc and roo) beneath the southern sky, which, after dinner, is dissected and explained with the help of a telescope. If you're more of a morning person, try

the similarly styled **Desert Awakenings 4WD Tour** (www.ayersrockresort.com.au/desert-awakenings; adult/child $168/130). Neither tour is suitable for children under 10 years.

Scenic Flights

Prices are quoted per person and include airport transfers from Ayers Rock Resort.

Ayers Rock Helicopters SCENIC FLIGHTS
(08-8956 2077; www.helicoptergroup.com/arh-index) A 15-minute buzz of Uluru costs $150; to include Kata Tjuta costs $285.

Kings Canyon & Watarrka National Park

The yawning chasm of Kings Canyon in Watarrka National Park is one of the most spectacular sights in central Australia, and one of the main attractions of the Mereenie Loop. The other ways to get here include the unsealed Ernest Giles Rd, which heads west off the Stuart Hwy 140km south of Alice Springs, and the sealed Luritja Rd which detours off the Lasseter Hwy on the way to Uluru. The latter is the longest route but easily the most popular and comfortable.

Whichever way you get here you will want to spend some time shaking off the road miles and taking in the scenery. Walkers are rewarded with awesome views on the **Kings Canyon Rim Walk** (see p20).

The **Kings Creek Walk** (2km return) is a short stroll along the rocky creek bed to a raised platform with views of the towering canyon rim.

About 10km east of the car park, the **Kathleen Springs Walk** (one hour, 2.6km return) is a pleasant wheelchair-accessible track leading to a waterhole at the head of a gorge.

The **Giles Track** (22km one-way, overnight) is a marked track that meanders along the George Gill Range between Kathleen Springs and the canyon; fill out the logbook at Reedy Creek rangers office so that in the event of an emergency, rangers can more easily locate you.

Tours

Several tour companies depart Alice and stop here on the way to/from Uluru.

Kings Creek Helicopters SCENIC FLIGHT
(08-8956 7474; www.kingscreekstation.com.au; flights per person $70-480) Flies from Kings Creek Station, including a breathtaking 30-minute canyon flight.

TED MEAD/GETTY IMAGES ©

Waterfall, Kings Canyon

Kings Canyon

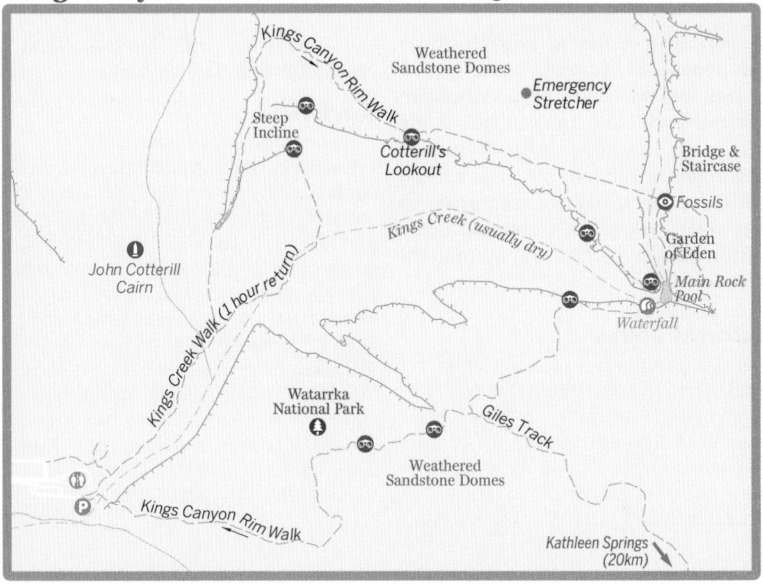

Professional Helicopter Services SCENIC FLIGHT
(PHS; ☎08-8956 2003; www.phs.com.au; flights per person $95-275) Picking up from Kings Canyon Resort, PHS buzzes the canyon for eight/15 minutes ($95/145).

Sleeping & Eating

Kings Creek Station CAMPING $$
(☎08-8956 7474; www.kingscreekstation.com.au; Luritja Rd; unpowered/powered sites for 2 people $40/44, safari cabins s/d incl breakfast $105/170; @ ≋) Located 35km before the canyon, this family-run station offers a bush camping experience among the desert oaks. The cosy safari-style cabins (small canvas tents on solid floors) share amenities and a kitchen-BBQ area. You can tear around the desert on a quad bike (one-hour ride $93) or enjoy the more sedate thrills of a sunset camel ride (one-hour ride $65).

Fuel, ice, beer, wine, BBQ packs and meals are available at the shop (open 7am to 7pm). Ask about Conways' Kids (www.conwayskids.org.au), a charitable trust set up by the owners to send local Indigenous children to school in Adelaide.

Kings Canyon Resort RESORT $$$
(☎08-8956 7442, 1300 863 248; www.kingscanyonresort.com.au; Luritja Rd; unpowered/powered sites $39/45, dm $35, d $285/469; ❄ @ ≈ ≋) Only 10km from the canyon, this well-designed resort boasts a wide range of accommodation, from a grassy camping area with its own pool and bar to deluxe rooms looking out onto native bushland. Eating and drinking options are as varied, with a bistro, the Thirsty Dingo bar and an outback BBQ for big steaks and live entertainment. There's a general store with fuel and an ATM at reception.

Kings Canyon Wilderness Lodge RESORT $$$
(☎1300 336 932; www.aptouring.com.au; Luritja Rd; tented cabins $640; ❄) In a secret pocket of Kings Creek Station is this luxury retreat with 10 stylish tents offering private en suite facilities and decks with relaxing bush views. It's run by APT, so independent travellers may find themselves squeezed in among tour groups. Tariff includes breakfast and dinner.

Indigenous Art & Culture

The intricate and mesmerising art, stories and dances of Australia's Aboriginal peoples resonate with a deep association with the land itself. The outback is the best place to engage with Aboriginal cuture: take a cultural tour, hear spoken stories of the Dreaming, see galleries of ancient rock art or check out some contemporary canvasses in modern acrylics.

Cultural Tours

There's a proliferation of Indigenous-owned and -operated cultural tours across outback Australia – a chance to learn about the outback from the people who know it best. Sign up for a cultural tour in Darwin, Kakadu National Park and Arnhem Land in the tropical north; and Alice Springs and Uluru-Kata Tjuta National Park in the red centre.

Rock Art

Evidence of Australia's ancient Indigenous culture can be found at the outdoor rock-art sites scattered across the outback. Highlights include the 5000-plus sites in Kakadu National Park that document a timeline of spirits from the Dreaming, extinct fauna, and remarkable 'contact art', portraying the interaction between Indigenous Australians, Macassan fishermen and early European settlers. Standout Kakadu sites include Ubirr and Nourlangie. More rock art can easily be seen at Nitmiluk and Keep River national parks, the MacDonnell Ranges near Alice, and Uluru.

1

Contemporary Indigenous Art

Contemporary Australian Indigenous art – the lion's share of which is produced in outback communities – has soared to global heights of late. Traditional methods and spiritual significance are fastidiously maintained, but often finding a counterpart in Western materials – the results can be wildly original interpretations of traditional stories and ceremonial designs. Dot paintings (acrylic on canvas) are the most recognisable form, but you may also see synthetic polymer paintings, weavings, barks, weapons, boomerangs and sculptures.

Indigenous Festivals

For an unforgettable Aboriginal cultural experience, time your outback visit to coincide with a traditional Indigenous festival. These celebrations offer visitors a look at Aboriginal culture in action. Witnessing a timeless dance and feeling the primal beats is a journey beyond time and place. The Northern Territory plays host to several Indigenous festivals and events, including the popular Walking With Spirits in Beswick, Barunga Festival near Katherine, Merrepen Arts Festival at Daly River, and Arnhem Land's Stone CountryFestival.

OLIVER STREWE/GETTY IMAGES ©

2

LEANNE WALKER/GETTY IMAGES ©

1. Dot painting, Northern Territory **2.** Barunga Festival, near Katherine (p71)

ALICE SPRINGS

POP 25,186

Alice Springs tends to evoke contradiction and polarises travellers – some love it and some hate it. But either way, you'll undoubtedly end up here at some point if you tour the Red Centre. The town has a lot to offer visitors, including a wide range of accommodation, excellent dining options and travel connections. For many travellers, Alice Springs is their first encounter with contemporary Indigenous Australia – with its enchanting art, mesmerising culture and present-day challenges.

This ruggedly beautiful town is shaped by its mythical landscapes, vibrant Aboriginal culture (where else can you hear six uniquely Australian languages in the main street?) and tough pioneering past. The town is a natural base for exploring central Australia, with Uluru-Kata Tjuta National Park a relatively short four-hour drive away. The mesmerising MacDonnell Ranges stretch east and west from the town centre, and you don't have to venture far to find yourself among ochre-red gorges, pastel-hued hills and ghostly white gum trees.

Sights

Alice Springs Desert Park WILDLIFE PARK
(☎08-8951 8788; www.alicespringsdesertpark.com.au; Larapinta Dr; adult/child $25/12.50; ⏱7.30am-6pm, last entry 4.30pm) If you haven't managed to glimpse a spangled grunter or marbled velvet gecko on your travels, head to the Desert Park where the creatures of central Australia are all on display in one place. The predominantly open-air exhibits faithfully re-create the animals' natural environments in a series of habitats: inland river, sand country and woodland.

It's an easy 2.5km cycle to the park. Alternatively, **Desert Park Transfers** (☎08-8952 1731; www.tailormadetours.com.au; adult/child $40/22) runs from Alice Springs five times daily. The cost includes park entry and pick-up/drop-off at your accommodation.

Try to time your visit with the terrific birds of prey show, featuring free-flying Australian kestrels, kites and awesome wedge-tailed eagles. To catch some of the park's rare and elusive animals, such as the bilby, visit the excellent nocturnal house. If you like what you see, come back at night and spotlight endangered species on the guided nocturnal tour (bookings essential).

To get the most out of the park pick up a free audioguide (available in various languages) or join one of the free ranger-led talks held throughout the day.

Araluen Cultural Precinct CULTURAL CENTRE
(☎08-8951 1122; http://artsandmuseums.nt.gov.au/araluen-cultural-precinct; cnr Larapinta Dr & Memorial Ave; precinct pass adult/child $15/10) The Araluen Cultural Precinct is Alice Springs' cultural hub; leave at least an afternoon aside for exploration of its excellent sights. You can wander around freely outside, accessing the cemetery and grounds, but the 'precinct pass' provides entry to the exhibitions and displays for two days (with 14 days to use the pass).

➡ **Araluen Arts Centre**
(☎08-8951 1122; http://artsandmuseums.nt.gov.au/araluen-cultural-precinct; cnr Larapinta Dr & Memorial Ave) For a small town, Alice Springs has a thriving arts scene, and the Araluen Arts Centre is at its heart. There is a 500-seat theatre (p67), and four galleries with a focus on art from the central desert region.

The Albert Namatjira Gallery features works by the artist, who began painting watercolours in the 1930s at Hermannsburg. The exhibition draws comparisons between Namatjira and his initial mentor, Rex Battarbee, and other Hermannsburg School artists. It also features 14 early acrylic works from the Papunya Community School Collection.

Other galleries showcase local artists, travelling exhibitions and newer works from Indigenous community art centres.

➡ **Museum of Central Australia**
(☎08-8951 1121; http://artsandmuseums.nt.gov.au/araluen-cultural-precinct; cnr Larapinta Dr & Memorial Ave; ⏱10am-5pm Mon-Fri) The natural history collection at this compact museum recalls the days of megafauna – when hippo-sized wombats and 3m-tall flightless birds roamed the land. Among the geological displays are meteorite fragments and fossils. There's a free audio tour, narrated by a palaeontologist, which helps bring the exhibition to life.

There's also a display on the work of Professor TGH Strehlow, a linguist and anthropologist born at the Hermannsburg Mission among the Arrernte people. During his lifetime he gathered one of the world's most documented collections of Australian Aboriginal artefacts, songs, genealogies, film and sound recordings. It's upstairs in the **Strehlow Research Centre**, which has a library open to the public.

GREG WOOD / STAFF/GETTY IMAGES ©

Dingos and keeper, Alice Springs Desert Park

➡ **Central Australia Aviation Museum** (www.centralaustralianaviationmuseum.com; Memorial Ave; ⏰10am-4pm Mon-Fri, 11am-4pm Sat & Sun) FREE Housed in the Connellan Airways Hangar are displays on pioneer aviation in the Northern Territory, including Royal Flying Doctor Service (RFDS) planes.

Easily the most interesting exhibit is the wreck of the *Kookaburra,* a tiny plane that crashed in the Tanami Desert in 1929 while searching for Charles Kingsford Smith and his co-pilot Charles Ulm, who had gone down in their plane, the *Southern Cross.* The *Kookaburra* pilots, Keith Anderson and Bob Hitchcock, perished in the desert, while Kingsford Smith and Ulm were rescued.

Royal Flying Doctor Service Base MUSEUM
(RFDS; ☎08-8958 8411; www.flyingdoctor.org.au; Stuart Tce; adult/child $12/6; ⏰9am-5pm Mon-Sat, 1-5pm Sun, cafe 8.30am-4.30pm Mon-Sat) A $3 million facelift, which includes interactive information portals, has given this excellent museum a new lease of life. It is the home of the Royal Flying Doctor Service, whose dedicated health workers provide 24-hour emergency retrievals across an area of around 1.25 million sq km. State-of-the-art facilities include a video presentation and a look at the operational control room, as well as some ancient medical gear and a flight simulator.

School of the Air MUSEUM
(☎08-8951-6834; www.assoa.nt.edu.au; 80 Head St; adult/child $7.50/5; ⏰8.30am-4.30pm Mon-Sat, 1-4.30pm Sun) Started in 1951, this was the first school of its type in Australia, broadcasting lessons to children over an area of 1.3 million sq km. While transmissions were originally all done over high-frequency radio, satellite broadband internet and web-cams now mean students can study in a virtual classroom. The guided tour of the centre includes a video. The school is about 3km north of the town centre.

Alice Springs Transport Heritage Centre MUSEUM
(www.roadtransporthall.com) At the MacDonnell siding, 10km south of Alice and 1km west of the Stuart Hwy, are a couple of museums dedicated to big trucks and old trains. The **Old Ghan Heritage Railway Museum** (☎08-8952 7161; 1 Norris Bell Dr; adult/child $10/6; ⏰9am-5pm) has a collection of restored *Ghan* locos, tea rooms, and a collection of railway memorabilia in the lovely Stuart railway station. For a truckin' good time, head to the **National Road Transport Hall of Fame** (www.roadtransporthall.com; 2 Norris Bell Ave; adult/child $15/8; ⏰9am-5pm) which has a fabulous collection of big rigs, including a few ancient road trains.

The transport hall of fame has more than 100 restored trucks and vintage cars, including many of the outback's pioneering vehicles. Admission includes entry to the Kenworth Dealer Truck Museum.

Alice Springs

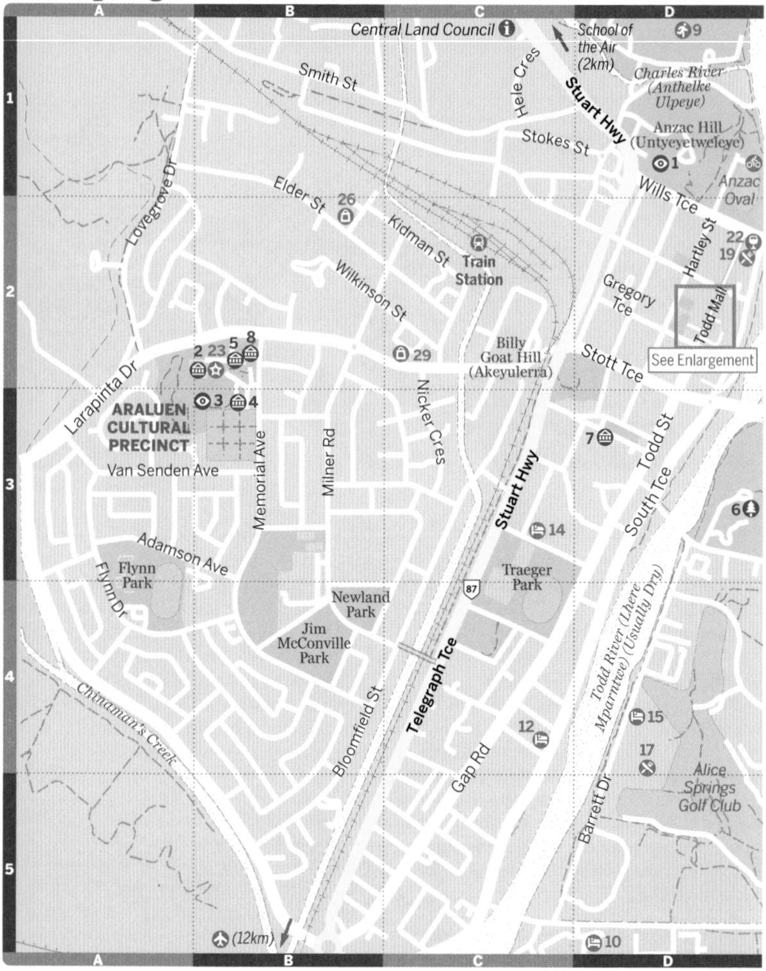

Olive Pink Botanic Garden NATURE RESERVE
(☎08-8952 2154; www.opbg.com.au; Tuncks Rd; admission by donation; ⏰8am-6pm) A network of meandering trails leads through this lovely arid zone botanic garden, which was founded by the prominent anthropologist Olive Pink. The garden has more than 500 central Australian plant species and grows bush foods and medicinal plants like native lemon grass, quandong and bush passionfruit.

There's a gentle climb up Meyers Hill with fine views over Alice and Ntyarlkarle Tyaneme, one of the first sites created by the caterpillar ancestors.

The small visitor centre has various exhibitions during the year, and the excellent **Bean Tree Cafe** (☎08-8952 0190; www.opbg.com.au/bean-tree-cafe; Tuncks Rd, Olive Pink Botanic Garden; mains $12-20; ⏰8am-4pm) alone is worth a trip to the gardens.

Anzac Hill LANDMARK
For a tremendous view, particularly at sunrise and sunset, take a hike (use Lions Walk from Wills Tce) or a drive up to the top of Anzac Hill, known as Untyeyetweleye in Arrernte. From the war memorial there is a 365-degree view over the town down to Heavitree Gap and the MacDonnell Ranges.

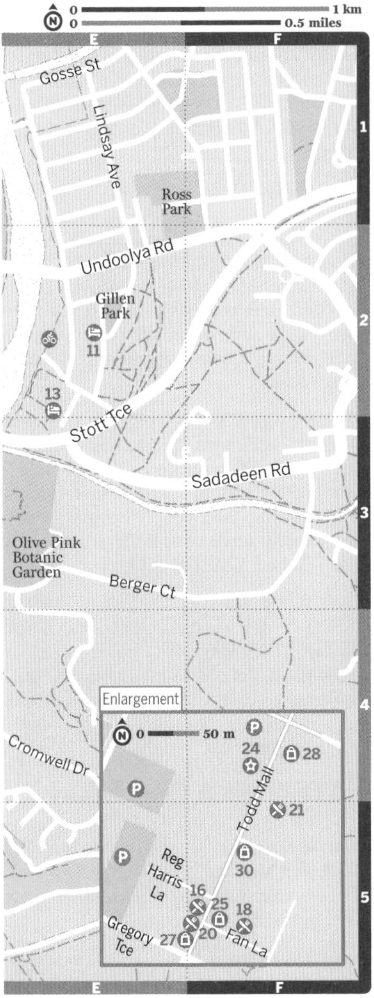

Alice Springs

Activities

Bushwalking

Experience the bush around Alice with several easy walks radiating from the Olive Pink Botanic Garden and the Telegraph Station.

Central Australian Bushwalkers BUSHWALKING
(http://centralaustralianbushwalkers.com; walks $5) A group of local bushwalkers that schedules a wide variety of walks in the area, particularly the West MacDonnell Ranges, from March to November.

Camel Riding

Camels played an integral part in pioneering central Australia before roads and railways, and travellers can relive some of that adventure.

Pyndan Camel Tracks CAMEL TOURS
(☎ 0416 170 1640; www.cameltracks.com; Jane Rd; 1hr rides adult/child $60/30) Local cameleer Marcus Williams offers one-hour rides, as well as half-day jaunts (per person $110).

Desert wattle, Ormiston Gorge (p68)
DIETER TRACEY/GETTY IMAGES ©

Cycling & Mountain-Bike Riding

Bikes are the perfect way to get around Alice Springs. There are cycle paths along the Todd River to the Telegraph Station, west to the Alice Springs Desert Park and further out to Simpsons Gap. For a map of cycling and walking paths go to the visitor information centre (p68).

Mountain bike trails are easily accessed from town, or meet up for a **social sunset ride** (☎08-8952 5800; centralaustralianroughriders.asn.au; rides $5) with the Central Australian Rough Riders' Club.

Outback Cycling BICYCLE RENTAL
(☎08-8952 3993; http://outbackcycling.com/alice-springs/bicycle-hire; Alice Springs Telegraph Station; day/week $30/140) Bike hire with urban and mountain bikes available, as well as baskets, kids' bikes and baby seats.

Tours

Around Alice & MacDonnell Ranges

Dreamtime Tours CULTURAL TOUR
(☎08-8953 3739; www.rstours.com.au; adult/child $85/42, self-drive $66/33; ⊙8.30-11.30am) Runs the three-hour Dreamtime & Bushtucker Tour, where you meet Warlpiri Aboriginal people and learn a little about their traditions. As it caters for large bus groups it can be impersonal, but you can tag along with your own vehicle.

Foot Falcon WALKING TOUR
(☎0427 569 531; http://footfalcon.wordpress.com; tours $30; ⊙4pm Mon-Fri, 3pm Sun) Local historian, author and teacher Linda Wells leads two-hour walks around town with insights into Alice's Indigenous and pioneering history.

Rainbow Valley Cultural Tours CULTURAL TOUR
(☎08-8956 0661; www.rainbowvalleyculturaltours.com; afternoon walking tours adult/child $80/50) Tour beautiful Rainbow Valley with a traditional owner and visit rock-art sites not open to the general public. Tours can include overnight camping and dinner for an extra $20.

RT Tours TOUR
(☎08-8952 0327; www.rttoursaustralia.com; tours $160) Chef and Arrernte guide Bob Taylor runs a popular lunch and dinner tour at Simpsons Gap and the Telegraph Station Historical Reserve, where he whips up a bush-inspired meal. Other tours available.

Trek Larapinta WALKING
(☎1300 133 278; www.treklarapinta.com.au; from 3/6 days $1195/2195) Guided multiday walks along sections of the Larapinta Trail. Also runs volunteer projects involving trail maintenance, and bush regeneration on Aboriginal outstations.

Festivals & Events

Alice Springs Cup Carnival HORSE RACING
(www.alicespringsturfclub.org.au) On the first Monday in May, don a hat and gallop down to the Pioneer Park Racecourse for the main event of this five-day carnival.

Finke Desert Race MOTOCROSS
(www.finkedesertrace.com.au) Motorcyclists and buggy drivers vie to take out the title of this crazy June race 240km from Alice along the Old South Rd to Finke; the following day they race back again. Spectators camp along the road to cheer them on.

Alice Springs Beanie Festival ARTS
(www.beaniefest.org) This four-day festival in June/July, held at the Araluen Arts Centre, celebrates the humble beanie (knitted woollen hat) – handmade by women throughout the central desert.

Camel Cup CAMEL RACING
(www.camelcup.com.au) A carnival atmosphere prevails during the running of the Camel Cup at Blatherskite Park in mid-July.

Alice Springs Rodeo
RODEO

Bareback bull riding, steer wrestling and ladies' barrel races are on the bill at Blatherskite Park in August.

Old Timers Fete
FETE

Stock up on doilies and tea towels at this ode to granny arts, held on the second Saturday in August at the Old Timers Village.

Alice Desert Festival
ART

(www.alicedesertfestival.com.au) A cracker of a festival, including a circus program, music, film and comedy. A colourful parade down Todd Mall marks the beginning of the festival. It's held in September.

🛏 Sleeping

If you are travelling in peak season (June to September) make sure you book ahead, but if you're trying your luck, check the internet for last-minute rates, which often bring top-end places into midrange reach.

Alice Lodge Backpackers
HOSTEL $

(☑1800 351 925, 08-8953 1975; www.alicelodge. com.au; 4 Mueller St; dm $24-26, d/tr $68/80; ❈@ 🛜 🌊) Alice Lodge gets great feedback from travellers, particularly for the friendly and helpful management. An easy 10-minute walk from town, this is a small, highly recommended, low-key hostel. Friendly staff are as accommodating as the variety of room options, which include mixed and female, three-, four- and six-bed dorms, as well as comfortable doubles and twins built around a central pool.

Alice's Secret Traveller's Inn
HOSTEL $

(☑08-8952 8686; www.asecret.com.au; 6 Khalick St; dm $23-26, s/d/tr $60/70/90; ❈@🌊) Get the best accommodation deals here by booking your tour to Uluru through the inn. One of our favourite hostels in Alice, just across the Todd River from town, this place gets a big thumbs up for cleanliness and the helpful, friendly owner. Relax around the pool, puff on a didgeridoo, or lie in a hammock in the garden.

Rooms in the dongas (temporary dwelling) are a bit of a squeeze, and those in the house are simple, comfortable and well kept.

Annie's Place
HOSTEL $

(☑08-8952 1545, 1800 359 089; www.anniesplace. com.au; 4 Traeger Ave; dm $22-25, d & tw $60-75; ❈@🌊) With its leafy beer garden – madly popular with travellers and locals alike – and great poolside area, Annie's is a lively place to hang out any night of the week. This is only a problem if you actually enjoy sleeping. The converted motel rooms (all with bathroom and some with a fridge) are a bit small, but they're cosy, and breakfast is included.

MacDonnell Range Holiday Park
CARAVAN PARK $

(☑1800 808 373, 08-8952 6111; www.macrange. com.au; Palm Pl; unpowered/powered sites $41/47, cabins d $100-230; ❈@🌊) Probably Alice's biggest and best kept, this caravan park has grassy sites and spotless amenities. Accommodation ranges from simple cabins with shared bathroom to self-contained two-bedroom villas. Kids can cavort in the adventure playground, on the BMX track and in the basketball court. Three new pools were to open in 2015.

Heavitree Gap Outback Lodge
CARAVAN PARK $

(☑1800 896 119, 08-8950 4444; www.aurorare-sorts.com.au; Palm Circuit; unpowered/powered sites $26/34, d $100-180; ❈@ 🛜 🌊) At the foot of the MacDonnell Ranges and dotted with eucalyptuses and bounding rock wallabies, Heavitree makes a shady place to pitch or park. There are rooms: a four-bed dorm, and a lodge with very basic kitchenette rooms that sleep six. The lodge offers a free shuttle into the town centre, which is about 4km north. The neighbouring tavern has live country music most nights of the week.

⭐ Alice in the Territory
RESORT $$

(☑08-8952 6100; www.alicent.com.au; 46 Stephens Rd; dm $25-35, s & d $110-150; ❈@ 🛜 🌊) One of the Alice's best-value accommodation options. Sure, it's a large sprawling resort, and the rooms are pretty straight up and down – doubles or four-bed dorms, with tiny bathrooms. But rooms are bright, spotless and comfortable.

There's great bar and a multicuisine restaurant, and the big pool sits at the foot of the MacDonnell Ranges.

Alice on Todd
APARTMENTS $$

(☑08-8953 8033; www.aliceontodd.com; cnr Strehlow St & South Tce; studio/1-bed apt $135/158; ❈@ 🛜 🌊) This place has a great set-up, with friendly and helpful staff. It's an attractive and secure apartment complex on the banks of the Todd River offering one- and two- bedroom self-contained units with kitchen and lounge. There are also studios. The balconied units sleep up to six so they're

Standley Chasm (Angkerle; p68), West MacDonnell Ranges
ANDREW BAIN/GETTY IMAGES ©

a great option for families. The landscaped grounds enclose a BBQ area, playground and games room.

Desert Palms Resort HOTEL $$
(☎08-8952 5977, 1800 678 037; www.desertpalms.com.au; 74 Barrett Dr; villas $140; ❄@≋) This hotel has a relaxed island vibe with palms, cascading bougainvillea and Indonesian-style villas. Rooms have cathedral ceilings, kitchenette, tiny bathroom, TV and private balcony – rather dated but comfy. The island swimming pool is a big hit with kids.

Eating

★Piccolo's CAFE $
(☎08-8953 1936; Shop 1, Cinema Complex 11, Todd Mall; breakfast $10-18; ⏱7.30am-3pm Mon-Fri, to 2pm Sat, 8am-1.30pm Sun) This modern, stylish cafe is popular with locals for its excellent food and probably Alice's best coffee. It wouldn't be out of place in Melbourne except service is faster and friendlier. The BRAT is recommended.

Page 27 Cafe CAFE $
(☎08-8952 0191; Fan Lane; mains $9-15; ⏱7.30am-2.30pm Tue-Fri, 8am-2pm Sat & Sun; 🖉) Alice's locals duck down this arcade for great coffee or fresh juice. There are wholesome home-style breakfasts (eggs any style, pancakes), pita wraps and fancy salads such as chicken fattoush, herbed quinoa, rocket and baba ganoush. Excellent vegetarian menu.

Epilogue Lounge TAPAS $$
(☎08-8953 4206; 58 Todd Mall; tapas/mains $15/25; ⏱8am-11.30pm Wed-Mon) This urban, retro delight is definitely the coolest place to hang in town. With a decent wine list, food served all day and service with a smile, it is a real Alice Springs standout. They hadn't quite honed some of their tapas dishes when we last visited – but a revamped menu was a work in progress.

Red Dog Cafe CAFE $$
(☎08-8953 1353; 64 Todd Mall; breakfast $12.50, lunch $16.50) There is no better place to people watch than here at one of the table and chairs strewn out over Todd Mall. Breakfasts are hearty, coffee is fresh and well brewed. Lunch is all about burgers, with a few veggie options thrown in.

★Hanuman Restaurant THAI $$
(☎08-8953 7188; www.hanuman.com.au/alice-springs; 82 Barrett Dr, Doubletree by Hilton; mains $25-36; ⏱12.30-2.30pm Mon-Fri, from 6.30pm daily; 🖉) You won't believe you're in the outback when you try the incredible Thai- and Indian-influenced cuisine at this stylish restaurant. The delicate Thai entrées are a real triumph as are the seafood dishes, particularly the Hanuman prawns. Although the menu is ostensibly Thai, there are enough Indian dishes to satisfy a curry craving. There are several vegetarian offerings and a good wine list.

Red Ochre Grill MODERN AUSTRALIAN $$$
(☎08-8952 9614; www.redochrealice.com.au; Todd Mall; lunch mains $15-18, dinner mains $30-37; ⏱10am-9pm) Offering innovative fusion dishes with a focus on outback cuisine, the menu here usually features traditional meats plus locally bred proteins, such as kangaroo and emu, matched with native herbs: lemon myrtle, pepperberries and bush tomatoes. There are lots of special deals such as tapas with a bottle of wine for $49, or 20% off for an early-bird dinner.

Drinking

Annie's Place BAR
(4 Traeger Ave; ⏱5pm-late) Bustling backpackers bar. Decent music (sometimes live),

leafy beer garden, cheap jugs and poolside drinking.

Todd Tavern PUB
(www.toddtavern.com.au; 1 Todd Mall; ⌚10am-midnight) This enduring, classically Aussie pub has a lively bar, pokies, decent pub grub and occasional live music on the weekend.

Entertainment

The gig guide in the entertainment section of the *Centralian Advocate* (published every Tuesday and Friday) lists what's on in and around town. Check out the Epilogue Lounge for some of Alice Spring's best live music on the weekend.

Araluen Arts Centre ARTS CENTRE
(☎08-8951 1122; http://artsandmuseums.nt.gov.au/araluen-cultural-precinct; Larapinta Dr) In the cultural heart of Alice, the 500-seat Araluen Theatre hosts a diverse range of performers, from dance troupes to comedians, while the Art House Cinema screens films every Sunday evening at 7pm (adult/child $15/12). The website has an events calendar.

Sounds of Starlight Theatre LIVE MUSIC
(☎08-8953 0826; www.soundsofstarlight.com; 40 Todd Mall; adult/concession/family $30/25/90; ⌚8pm Tue, Fri & Sat) This atmospheric 1½-hour musical performance evoking the spirit of the outback with didgeridoo, drums and keyboards, plus wonderful photography and lighting, is an Alice institution. Musician Andrew Langford also runs free didgeridoo lessons (11am Monday to Friday).

Shopping

Alice is the centre for Aboriginal arts from all over central Australia. The places owned and run by community art centres ensure that a better slice of the proceeds goes to the artist and artist's community. Look for the black over red Indigenous Art Code (www.indigenousartcode.org) displayed by dealers dedicated to fair and transparent dealings with artists.

Talapi ARTS
(☎08-8953 6389; http://talapi.com.au; 45 Todd Mall) One of Alice Spring's newest galleries, Talapi is a beautiful space in the heart of town, exhibiting and promoting central desert Indigenous art. It sources its artworks directly from Aboriginal-owned art centres and is a member of the Indigenous Art Code. Drop in to ask about upcoming exhibitions.

Aboriginal Art World ARTS
(☎08-8952 7788; www.aboriginalartworld.com.au; 89 Todd Mall) Specialises in art from artists living in the central desert region around Alice Springs, particularly Pitjantjatjara lands. You can buy a completed work or commission your own piece.

Desert Dwellers OUTDOOR EQUIPMENT
(☎08-8953 2240; www.desertdwellers.com.au; 38 Elder St; ⌚9am-5pm Mon-Fri, to 2pm Sat) For camping and hiking gear, head to this shop, which has just about everything you need to equip yourself for an outback jaunt – maps, swags, tents, portable fridges, stoves and more.

Mbantua Gallery ARTS
(☎08-8952 5571; www.mbantua.com.au; 64 Todd Mall; ⌚9am-6pm Mon-Fri, to 1pm Sat, 10am-1pm Sun) This privately owned gallery includes extensive exhibits of works from the renowned Utopia region, as well as watercolour landscapes from the Namatjira school. There is a superb cultural exhibition space here with panels explaining Aboriginal mythology and customs.

Tjanpi Desert Weavers ARTS
(☎08-8958 2377; www.tjanpi.com.au; 3 Wilkinson St; ⌚10am-4pm Mon-Fri) This small enterprise employs and supports central desert weavers from 18 remote communities. Their store is well worth a visit to see the magnificent woven baskets and quirky sculptures created from locally collected grasses.

Todd Mall Market MARKET
(www.toddmallmarkets.com.au; ⌚9am-1pm or 2pm) Buskers, craft stalls, sizzling woks, smoky satay stands, Aboriginal art, jewellery and knick-knacks make for a relaxed stroll. The market runs two to three times monthly – check the website for dates.

Information

Dangers & Annoyances

Avoid walking alone at night anywhere in town. Catch a taxi back to your accommodation if you're out late.

Emergency

Ambulance (☎000) For emergencies.

Internet Access

Travel Bug (19 Todd Mall; 24min $2) Internet access.

Medical Services

Alice Springs Hospital (08-8951 7777; www.health.nt.gov.au/hospitals/alice_springs_hospital; Gap Rd) For medical care.

Money

Major banks with ATMs, such as ANZ, Commonwealth, National Australia and Westpac, are located in and around Todd Mall in the town centre.

Post

Main Post Office (13 13 18; 31-33 Hartley St; 8.15am-5pm Mon-Fri) All the usual services are available here.

Tourist Information

Central Land Council (08-8951 6211; www.clc.org.au; PO Box 3321, 27 Stuart Hwy, Alice Springs; 8.30am-noon & 2-4pm) For Aboriginal land permits and transit permits.

Tourism Central Australia Visitor Information Centre (1800 645 199, 08-8952 5199; www.discovercentralaustralia.com; cnr Todd Mall & Parsons St; 8.30am-5pm Mon-Fri, 9.30am-4pm Sat & Sun;) This helpful centre can load you up with stacks of brochures and the free visitors guide. Weather forecasts and road conditions are posted on the wall. National parks information is also available. Ask about their unlimited kilometre deals if you are thinking of renting a car.

Getting There & Away

CAR & MOTORCYCLE

Alice Springs is a long way from everywhere. It's 1180km to Mt Isa in Queensland, 1490km to Darwin and 441km (4½ hours) to Yulara (for Uluru). Although the roads to the north and south are sealed and in good condition, these are still outback roads, and it's wise to have your vehicle well prepared, particularly as you won't get a mobile phone signal outside Alice or Yulara. Carry plenty of drinking water and emergency food at all times.

West MacDonnell Ranges

With their stunning beauty and rich diversity of plants and animals, the West MacDonnell Ranges are not to be missed. Their easy access by conventional vehicle makes them especially popular with day-trippers. Heading west from Alice, Namatjira Dr turns northwest off Larapinta Dr 6km beyond Standley Chasm and is sealed all the way to Tylers Pass.

Most sites in the West MacDonnell Ranges lie within the **West MacDonnell National Park**, except for Standley Chasm, which is privately owned. There are ranger stations at Simpsons Gap and Ormiston Gorge.

Simpsons Gap

Westbound from Alice Springs on Larapinta Dr you come to the grave of **John Flynn**, the founder of the Royal Flying Doctor Service, which is topped by a boulder donated by the Arrernte people (the original was a since-returned Devil's Marble). Opposite the car park is the start of the sealed **cycling track** to Simpsons Gap, a recommended three- to four-hour return ride.

By road, **Simpsons Gap** is 22km from Alice Springs and 8km off Larapinta Dr. It's a popular picnic spot and has some excellent short walks. Early morning and late afternoon are the best times to glimpse black-footed rock wallabies. The visitor information centre is 1km from the park entrance.

Standley Chasm (Angkerle)

About 50km west of Alice Springs is the spectacular **Standley Chasm** (08-8956 7440; adult/concession $10/8; 8am-5pm, last chasm entry 4.30pm), which is owned and run by the nearby community of Iwupataka. There's a cafe, picnic facilities and toilets near the car park. For more, see p21.

Namatjira Drive

Namatjira Dr takes you to a whole series of gorges and gaps in the West MacDonnell Ranges. Not far beyond Standley Chasm you can choose the northwesterly Namatjira Dr (which loops down to connect with Larapinta Dr west of Hermannsburg), or you can continue along Larapinta Dr.

If you choose Namatjira Dr, one of your first stops might be **Ellery Creek Big Hole**, 91km from Alice Springs, and with a large permanent waterhole – a popular place for a swim on a hot day (the water is usually freezing). About 11km further, a rough gravel track leads to narrow, ochre-red **Serpentine Gorge**, which has a lovely waterhole blocking the entrance and a lookout at the end of a short, steep track (30 minutes, return), where you can view ancient cycads.

The **Ochre Pits** line a dry creek bed 11km west of Serpentine and were a source of pigment for Aboriginal people. The various coloured ochres – mainly yellow, white and red-brown – are weathered limestone, with iron oxide creating the colours.

ANDREW BAIN/GETTY IMAGES ©

Simpsons Gap

The car park for the majestic **Ormiston Gorge** is 25km beyond the Ochre Pits. It's the most impressive chasm in the West MacDonnells. There's a waterhole shaded with ghost gums, and the gorge curls around to the enclosed **Ormiston Pound**. It is a haven for wildlife and you can expect to see some critters among the spinifex slopes and mulga woodland. There are **walking tracks**, including the **Ghost Gum Lookout** (20 minutes), which affords brilliant views down the gorge, and the excellent, circuitous **Pound Walk** (three hours, 7.5km). There's a **visitor centre** (08-8956 7799; 10am-4pm) and a **kiosk**.

About 2km further is the turn-off to **Glen Helen Gorge**, where the Finke River cuts through the MacDonnells. Only 1km past Glen Helen is a good **lookout** over Mt Sonder; sunrise and sunset here are particularly impressive.

If you continue northwest for 25km you'll reach the turn-off (4WD only) to multihued, cathedral-like **Redbank Gorge**. This permanent waterhole runs for kilometres through the labyrinthine gorge, and makes for an incredible swimming and scrambling adventure on a hot day. Namatjira Dr then heads south and is sealed as far as **Tylers Pass Lookout**, which provides a dramatic view of **Tnorala** (Grosse Bluff), the legacy of an earth-shattering comet impact.

Sleeping & Eating

There are basic **camping grounds** (adult/child $5/1.50) at Ellery Creek Big Hole, Redbank Gorge and 6km west of Serpentine Gorge at Serpentine Chalet (a 4WD or high-clearance 2WD vehicle is recommended to reach the chalet ruins). The ritzy **camping area** (adult/child $10/5) at Ormiston Gorge has showers, toilets, gas barbecues and picnic tables.

Glen Helen Resort HOTEL **$**
(08-8956 7489; www.glenhelen.com.au; Namatjira Dr; unpowered/powered sites $24/35, dm/r $35/170;) At the edge of the West MacDonnell National Park is the popular Glen Helen Resort, which has an idyllic back verandah slammed up against the red ochre cliffs of the spectacular gorge. There's a busy restaurant-pub serving hearty meals and live music on the weekend. There are also 4WD tours available and helicopter flights.

There's a good chance you'll spot flocks of colourful budgerigars here while enjoying a cold drink in the evening. Pitching a tent on a grassy patch with your own campfire is a delight.

North to Darwin

The remote and largely untamed chunk of the Northern Territory from Alice Springs to Darwin is where dreams end and adventure begins. Explore this ancient land of escarpments, canyons, gorges and pockets of verdant bush.

Tennant Creek

POP 3061

Tennant Creek is the only town of any size between Katherine, 680km to the north, and Alice Springs, 511km to the south. It's a good place to break up a long drive and check out the town's few attractions. Tennant Creek is known as Jurnkurakurr to the local Warumungu people and almost half of the population is of Aboriginal descent.

Sights & Activities

Nyinkka Nyunyu GALLERY

(☎08-8962 2699; www.nyinkkanyunyu.com.au; Paterson St; tour guide $15; ⏰9am-5pm Mon-Fri, 10am-2pm Sat & Sun Oct-Apr, 8am-6pm Mon-Sat, 10am-2pm Sun May-Sep) This innovative museum and gallery highlights the dynamic art and culture of the local Warumungu people. The absorbing displays focus on contemporary art, traditional objects (many returned from interstate museums), bush medicine and regional history. The diorama series, or bush TVs as they became known within the community, are particularly special.

Nyinkka Nyunyu is located beside a sacred site of the spiky tailed goanna. Learn about bush tucker and Dreaming stories with your personal guide. There's also a gallery store and the lovely Jajjikari Café, which serves espresso coffee and light meals.

Battery Hill Mining Centre MINE

(☎08-8962 1281; www.barklytourism.com.au; Peko Rd; adult/child $25/15; ⏰9am-5pm) Experience life in Tennant Creek's 1930s gold rush at this mining centre, which doubles as the Visitor Information Centre, 2km east of town. There are **underground mine tours** and audio tours of the 10-head **battery**. In addition there is a superb **Minerals Museum** and you can try your hand at gold panning. The admission price gives access to all of the above, or you can choose to visit the Minerals and Social History Museums only (adult/family $7/15), or just go panning (per person $2).

While you're here, ask for the key ($20 refundable deposit) to the old Telegraph Station, which is just off the highway about 12km north of town. This is one of only four of the original 11 stations remaining in the Territory. Just north of the Telegraph Station is the turn-off west to Kundjarra (The Pebbles), a formation of granite boulders like a miniature version of the better-known Devil's Marbles found 100km south. It's a sacred women's Dreaming site of the Warumungu.

Sleeping & Eating

Tourist's Rest Youth Hostel HOSTEL $

(☎08-8962 2719; www.touristrest.com.au; cnr Leichhardt & Windley Sts; dm/d $30/65; ❄@≋) This small, friendly and slightly ramshackle hostel has bright clean rooms, free breakfast and VIP discounts. The hostel can organise tours of the gold mines and Devil's Marbles, plus pick-ups from the bus stop.

Outback Caravan Park CAMPGROUND $
(☎08-8962 2459; Peko Rd; unpowered/powered sites $15/36, cabins $70-150; ❄🏊) In a town that often feels parched, it's nice to be in the shade of this grassy caravan park about 1km east of the centre. There's a well-stocked kiosk, camp kitchen and fuel. You may even be treated to some bush poetry and bush tucker, courtesy of yarn spinner Jimmy Hooker, at 7.30pm ($5). Decent outdoor bar area, but be quick, as it closes early.

Safari Lodge Motel MOTEL $$
(☎08-8962 2207; http://safari.budgetmotelchain.com.au; Davidson St; s/d $110/130; ❄@📶) You should book ahead to stay at this family-run motel. Safari Lodge is centrally located next to the best restaurant in town and has clean, fairly standard rooms with phone, fridge and TV.

Top of the Town Cafe CAFE $
(☎08-8962 1311; 163 Paterson St; breakfast $7-14; ⏲7am-3pm Mon-Fri, to 1pm Sat) Home of pinkmolly cupcakes, this little gem is slightly twee. It's cute, quirky and a little cramped inside, but there are tables and chairs on the footpath too. There are a range of toasties and bacon-and-egg options for brekky, making it the best place in town for breakfast.

Woks Up CHINESE $$
(☎08-8962 3888; 108 Paterson St; mains $14-24; ⏲5pm-late) The clean, modern dining room, backed by delicious, tasty food with clean flavours, makes Woks Up one of the Territory's best Chinese diners. Generous portions of stir-fry in satay, Mongolian or black-bean sauce.

Information

Leading Edge Computers (☎08-8962 3907; 145 Paterson St; per 20min $2; ⏲9am-5.30pm Mon-Wed & Fri, to 7pm Thu, to noon Sat; 📶) Internet access.

Police Station (☎08-8962 4444; Paterson St) The town police station.

Tennant Creek Hospital (☎08-8962 4399; Schmidt St) For medical emergencies.

Visitor Information Centre (☎1800 500 879; www.barklytourism.com.au; Peko Rd; ⏲9am-5pm Mon-Fri, to 1pm Sat) Located 2km east of town at Battery Hill.

Daly Waters

POP 25

About 3km off the highway and 160km south of Mataranka is Daly Waters, an important staging post in the early days of aviation – aviator Amy Johnson landed here on her epic flight from England to Australia in 1930. Just about everyone stops at the famous **Daly Waters Pub** (see p29). It has become a bit of a legend along the Stuart Highway, although it may be a bit too popular for its own good. Every evening from April to September there's an Australiana show with host Chilli, often supported by local musicians. Hearty meals (mains $12 to $30, open lunch and dinner), including the filling barra burger, are served. Beside the pub is a dustbowl camping ground with a bit of shade – book ahead or arrive early to secure a powered site. Accommodation ranges from basic dongas (small, transportable buildings) to spacious self-contained cabins.

Katherine

POP 9187

Katherine is considered a big town in this part of the world and you'll certainly feel like you've arrived somewhere if you've just made the long trip up the highway from Alice Springs. Its namesake river is the first permanent running water on the road north of Alice Springs. Katherine is probably best known for the Nitmiluk (Katherine Gorge) National Park to the east, and the town makes an obvious base, with plenty of accommodation.

Sights & Activities

Godinymayin Yijard Rivers Arts & Culture Centre GALLERY
(☎08-8972 3751; www.gyracc.org.au; Stuart Hwy, Katherine East; ⏲10am-5pm Tue-Fri, to 3pm Sat) This stunning new arts and culture centre in Katherine is housed in a beautiful, contemporary building that is a real landmark for the town. The centre is designed to be a meeting place for Indigenous and non-Indigenous people, and a chance to share cultures – you can listen to locals share their stories on multimedia screens. Don't miss this place when you're in town. It's 1km south of Katherine, just after the public swimming pool.

Katherine

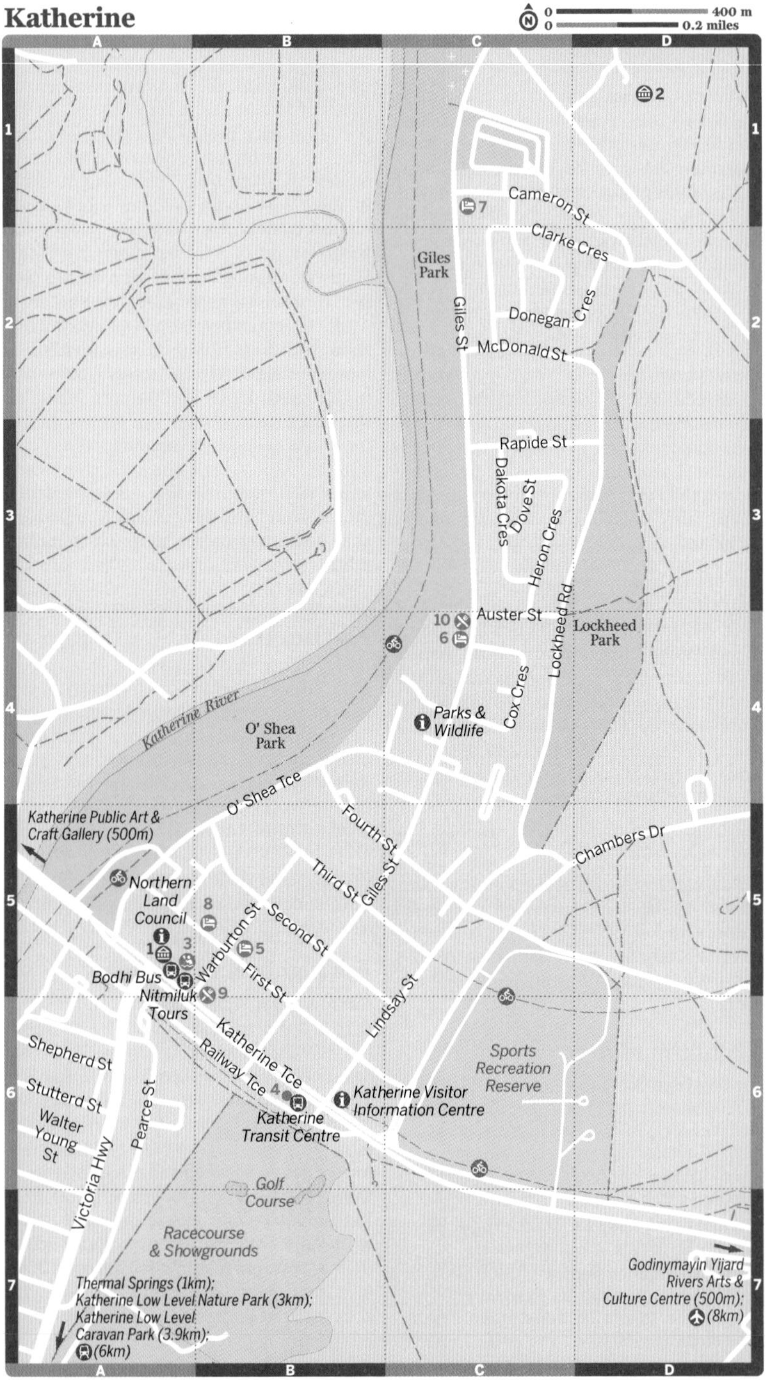

0 400 m
0 0.2 miles
A
B
C
D
1
2
3
4
5
6
7
2
Cameron St
7
Clarke Cres
Giles Park
Giles St
Donegan
Cres
McDonald St
Rapide St
Dakota Cres
Dove St
Heron Cres
Auster St
10
6
Lockheed Rd
Lockheed Park
Cox Cres
Parks & Wildlife
Katherine River
O' Shea Park
O' Shea Tce
Fourth St
Katherine Public Art & Craft Gallery (500m)
Chambers Dr
Northern Land Council
Third St
Giles St
8
Second St
1
3
Warburton St
5
Bodhi Bus
Nitmiluk Tours
9
First St
Lindsay St
Sports Recreation Reserve
Shepherd St
Katherine Tce
Railway Tce
Stutterd St
Walter Young St
Pearce St
4
Katherine Transit Centre
Katherine Visitor Information Centre
Victoria Hwy
Golf Course
Racecourse & Showgrounds
Thermal Springs (1km); Katherine Low Level Nature Park (3km); Katherine Low Level Caravan Park (3.9km); (6km)
Godinymayin Yijard Rivers Arts & Culture Centre (500m); (8km)

Katherine

Sights

Activities, Courses & Tours

Sleeping

Eating

The centre houses a beautiful gallery space hosting Territory artworks, and a performing arts venue seating up to 400 people.

Top Didj Cultural Experience & Art Gallery GALLERY
(☎08-8971 2751; www.topdidj.com; cnr Gorge & Jaensch Rds; cultural experience adult/child/family $65/45/200; ⏲cultural experience 9.30am & 2.30pm Sun-Fri, 9.30am & 1.30pm Sat) Run by the owners of the Katherine Art Gallery, Top Didj is a good place to see Aboriginal artists at work. The cultural experience is hands-on with fire sticks, spear throwing, painting and basket weaving.

Katherine Museum MUSEUM
(☎08-8972 3945; www.katherinemuseum.com; Gorge Rd; adult/child $10/4; ⏲9am-4pm) The museum is in the old airport terminal, about 3km from town on the road to the gorge. The original Gypsy Moth biplane flown by Dr Clyde Fenton, the first Flying Doctor, is housed here, along with plenty of interesting old rusty trucks. There's a good selection of historical photos, including a display on the 1998 flood.

Tours

Gecko Canoeing & Trekking OUTDOORS
(☎1800 634 319, 0427 067 154; www.geckocanoeing.com.au) Exhilarating guided canoe trips on the more remote stretches of the Katherine River. Trips include three days ($860) on the Katherine River and six days ($1600) on the Daly and Katherine Rivers. A five-day hike along the Jatbula Trail in Nitmiluk National Park costs $1600. Gecko can also shuttle Jatbula Trail hikers from Leliyn back to Katherine or Nitmiluk National Park HQ. Minimum numbers apply.

Crocodile Night Adventure CRUISE
(☎1800 089 103; www.travelnorth.com.au; adult/child $75/49; ⏲6.30pm May-Oct) At Springvale Homestead, this evening cruise seeks out crocs and other nocturnal wildlife on the Katherine River. Includes BBQ dinner and drinks.

Travel North SIGHTSEEING
(☎08-8971 9999, 1800 089 103; www.travelnorth.com.au; 6 Katherine Tce, Transit Centre) Katherine-based tour operator with a range of tours to Kakadu, Arnhem Land and Litchfield, and full-day Katherine town tours. Also booking agent for the Ghan and Greyhound.

Festivals & Events

Katherine Country Music Muster MUSIC
(www.kcmm.com.au; adult/child $35/free) 'We like both kinds of music: country *and* western.' Plenty of live music in the pubs and entertainment at the Tick Market Lindsay St Complex on a weekend in May or June. Check the website for actual dates.

Sleeping

Coco's Backpackers HOSTEL $
☎08-8971 2889; coco@21firstst.com.au; 21 First St; camping per person $20, dm $35) Travellers love this place, with Indigenous art on the walls and didgeridoos in the tin shed next door helping to provide an authentic Katherine experience. Coco's is a converted home where the owner chats with the guests and has great knowledge about the town and local area. Aboriginal artists are often here painting didgeridoos.

Katherine Low Level Caravan Park CARAVAN PARK $
(☎08-8972 3962; http://katherine-low-level-caravan-park.nt.big4.com.au; Shadforth Rd; unpowered/powered sites $37/40, safari tent $90; ❄📶🏊) A well-manicured park with plenty of shady sites, a great swimming pool adjoining a bar and an excellent bistro (mains $22 to $27) that is sheltered by a magnificent fig tree. The amenities are first rate, making it the pick of the town's several caravan parks. It's about 5km along the Victoria Hwy from town and across the Low Level bridge.

Knott's Crossing Resort MOTEL $$
(☎08-8972 2511; www.knottscrossing.com.au; cnr Cameron & Giles Sts; unpowered/powered sites $27/43, cabin/motel d from $110/160;

ANDREW WATSON/GETTY IMAGES ©

Kayaking in Katherine Gorge

) Probably the pick of Katherine's accommodation options. There is variety to suit most budgets; a fantastic restaurant; and the whole place is very professionally run. Everything is packed pretty tightly into the tropical gardens at Knott's, but it's easy to find your own little nook. It's also on the way to Katherine Gorge, giving you a head start if you want to get there early.

Katherine River Lodge Motel MOTEL **$$**
(08-8971 0266; http://katherineriverlodge.com.au; 50 Giles St; d/f from $120/180;) The rooms here recently underwent a facelift. While the service could do with a facelift too, the rooms are secure, have a modern touch and are well kept. This large complex (three three-storey blocks) in a tropical garden is particularly recommended for families, as there are interconnecting rooms available. The attached restaurant serves up excellent tucker.

St Andrews Apartments APARTMENTS **$$$**
(1800 686 106, 08-8971 2288; www.standrews-apts.com.au; 27 First St; apt $230-285;) In the heart of town, these serviced apartments are great for families and those pining for a few home comforts. The two-bedroom apartments sleep four (six if you use the sofa bed), and come with fully equipped kitchen and lounge/dining area. Nifty little BBQ decks are attached to the ground-floor units.

Eating

Coffee Club CAFE **$**
(www.coffeeclub.com.au; cnr Katherine Tce & Warburton St; meals $12-20; 6.30am-5pm Mon-Fri, 7am-4pm Sat & Sun) This is the best place in town for breakfast, as well as being a good bet at lunchtime. Dining is in a light-filled contemporary space. On offer is decent coffee, healthy breakfast options including fruit and muesli, plus burgers, sandwiches, wraps and salads all day.

★ **Escarpment Restaurant** MODERN AUSTRALIAN **$$**
(08-8971 1600; 50 Giles St; lunch $12, dinner $25; 11.30am-2.30pm & 5-10pm Mon-Sat) The exceedingly nice outdoor area, apart from its view of the car park, makes outdoor dining here very tempting. Happily the food backs the aesthetics. Lunches consist of burgers, wraps, salads and seafood dishes, with food preparation and presentation a step above most other places in town.

Savannah Bar & Restaurant MODERN AUSTRALIAN **$$**
(08-8972 2511; www.knottscrossing.com.au/restaurant; cnr Giles & Cameron Sts, Knott's Crossing Resort; mains $25-35; 6.30-9am & 6-9pm) Undoubtedly one of the best dining choices in Katherine. It's predominantly an outdoors garden restaurant, with a cool breeze often wafting through the tropical vegetation. The menu includes steak, barramundi

and Venus Bay prawn dishes. There's even a suckling pig you can tuck into. Service is fast and friendly, and the whole place is very well run.

Information

Katherine Hospital (08-8973 9211; www.health.nt.gov.au; Giles St) About 3km north of town, with an emergency department.

Katherine Visitor Information Centre (1800 653 142; www.visitkatherine.com.au; cnr Lindsay St & Stuart Hwy; 8.30am-5pm daily in the Dry, 8.30am-5pm Mon-Fri, 10am-2pm Sat & Sun in the Wet) Modern, air-con information centre stocking information on all areas of the Northern Territory. Pick up the handy *Katherine Region Visitor Guide*.

Parks & Wildlife 08-8973 8888; www.parksandwildlife.nt.gov.au; 32 Giles St; 8am-4.20pm) National park information and notes.

Getting There & Around

Katherine is a major road junction: from here the Stuart Hwy tracks north and south, and the Victoria Hwy heads west to Kununurra in Western Australia.

DARWIN

08 / POP 127,500

Darwin has plenty to offer the traveller. Chairs and tables spill out of streetside restaurants and bars, innovative museums celebrate the city's past, and galleries showcase the region's rich Indigenous art. Darwin's cosmopolitan mix – more than 50 nationalities are seamlessly represented here – is typified by the wonderful markets held throughout the dry season.

Nature is well and truly part of Darwin's backyard; the famous national parks of Kakadu and Litchfield are only a few hours' drive away, and the unique Tiwi Islands are a boat ride away. For locals the perfect weekend is going fishing for barra in a tinny (small boat) with an esky full of cold beer.

Sights

★Crocosaurus Cove ZOO

(08-8981 7522; www.crocosauruscove.com; 58 Mitchell St; adult/child $32/20; 9am-6pm, last admission 5pm) If the tourists won't go out to see the crocs, then bring the crocs to the tourists. Right in the middle of Mitchell St, Crocosaurus Cove is as close as you'll ever want to get to these amazing creatures. Six of the largest crocs in captivity can be seen in state-of-the-art aquariums and pools. Other aquariums feature barramundi, turtles and stingrays, plus there's an enormous reptile house (allegedly displaying the greatest variety of reptiles in the country).

You can be lowered right into a pool with the crocs in the transparent Cage of Death (one/two people $160/240). If that's too scary, there's another pool where you can swim with a clear tank wall separating you from some mildly less menacing baby crocs.

George Brown Botanic Gardens GARDENS

(http://www.parksandwildlife.nt.gov.au/botanic; Geranium St, Stuart Park; 7am-7pm, information centre 8am-4pm) FREE Named after the gardens' curator from 1971 to 1990, these 42-hectare gardens showcase plants from the Top End and around the world – monsoon vine forest, the mangroves and coastal plants habitat, boabs, and a magnificent collection of native and exotic palms and cycads.

The gardens are an easy 2km bicycle ride out from Darwin, along Gilruth Ave and Gardens Rd, or there's another entrance off Geranium St, which runs off the Stuart Hwy in Stuart Park. Alternatively, bus 7 from the city stops near the Stuart Hwy/Geranium St corner.

Many of the plants here were traditionally used by the local Aboriginal people, and self-guiding Aboriginal plant-use trails have been set up; pick up a brochure at the gardens' information centre near the Geranium St entry. You'll also find birdwatching brochures and garden maps here.

Myilly Point Heritage Precinct HISTORIC SITE

At the far northern end of Smith St is this small but important precinct of four houses built from 1930 to 1939 (which means they survived both the WWII bombings and Cyclone Tracy!). They're now managed by the National Trust. One of them, **Burnett House** (www.nationaltrustnt.org.au; admission by donation; 10am-1pm Mon-Sat, 2.30-5pm Sun), operates as a museum. There's a tantalising **colonial high tea** ($10) in the gardens on Sunday afternoon from 3pm between April and October.

Darwin Waterfront Precinct

The bold redevelopment of the old **Darwin Waterfront Precinct** (www.waterfront.nt.gov.au) has transformed the city. The

Darwin

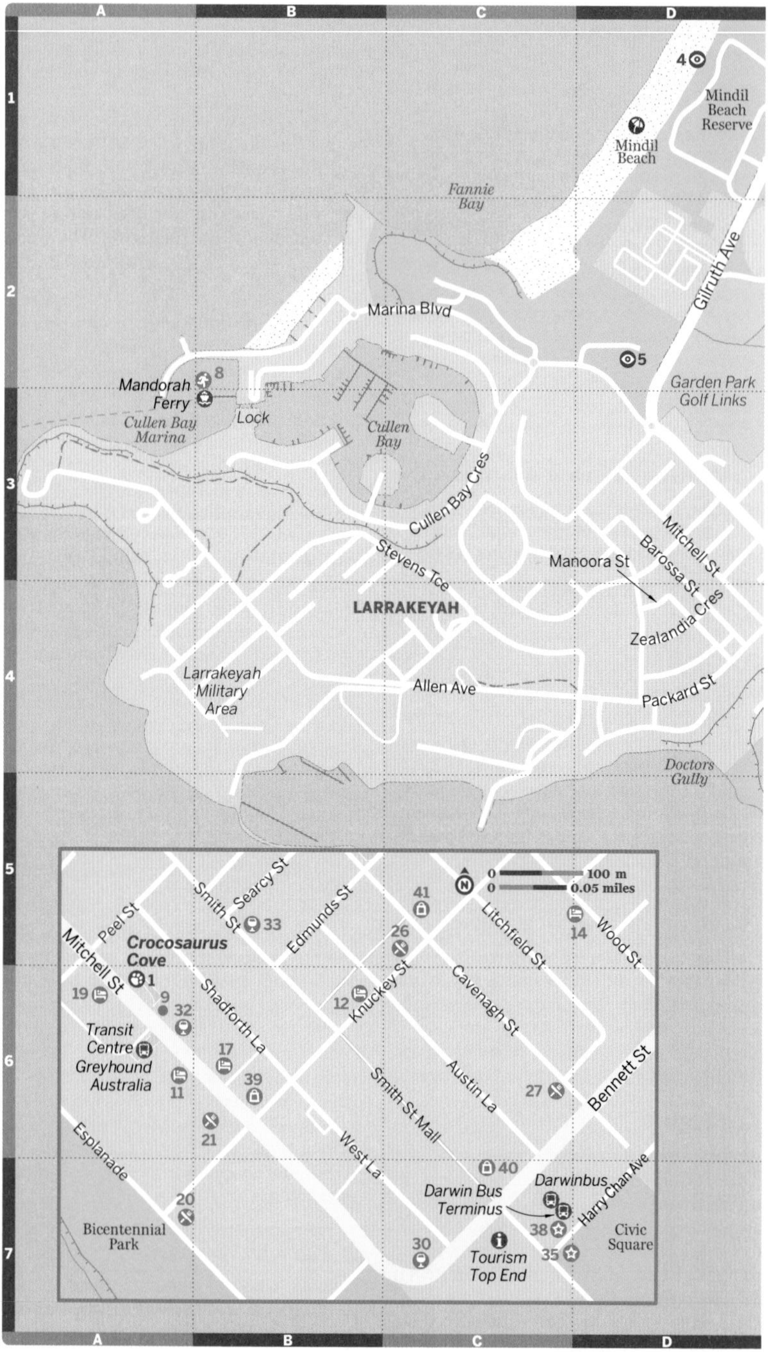

Mindil Beach Reserve
Mindil Beach
Fannie Bay
Gilruth Ave
Marina Blvd
Mandorah Ferry
Cullen Bay Marina
Lock
Cullen Bay
Garden Park Golf Links
Cullen Bay Cres
Stevens Tce
Manoora St
Mitchell St
Barossa St
Zealandia Cres
LARRAKEYAH
Larrakeyah Military Area
Allen Ave
Packard St
Doctors Gully
100 m
0.05 miles
Peel St
Smith St
Searcy St
Edmunds St
Litchfield St
Wood St
Mitchell St
Crocosaurus Cove
Shadforth La
Knuckey St
Cavenagh St
Transit Centre
Greyhound Australia
Smith St Mall
Austin La
Bennett St
Esplanade
West La
Darwin Bus Terminus
Darwinbus
Harry Chan Ave
Bicentennial Park
Tourism Top End
Civic Square

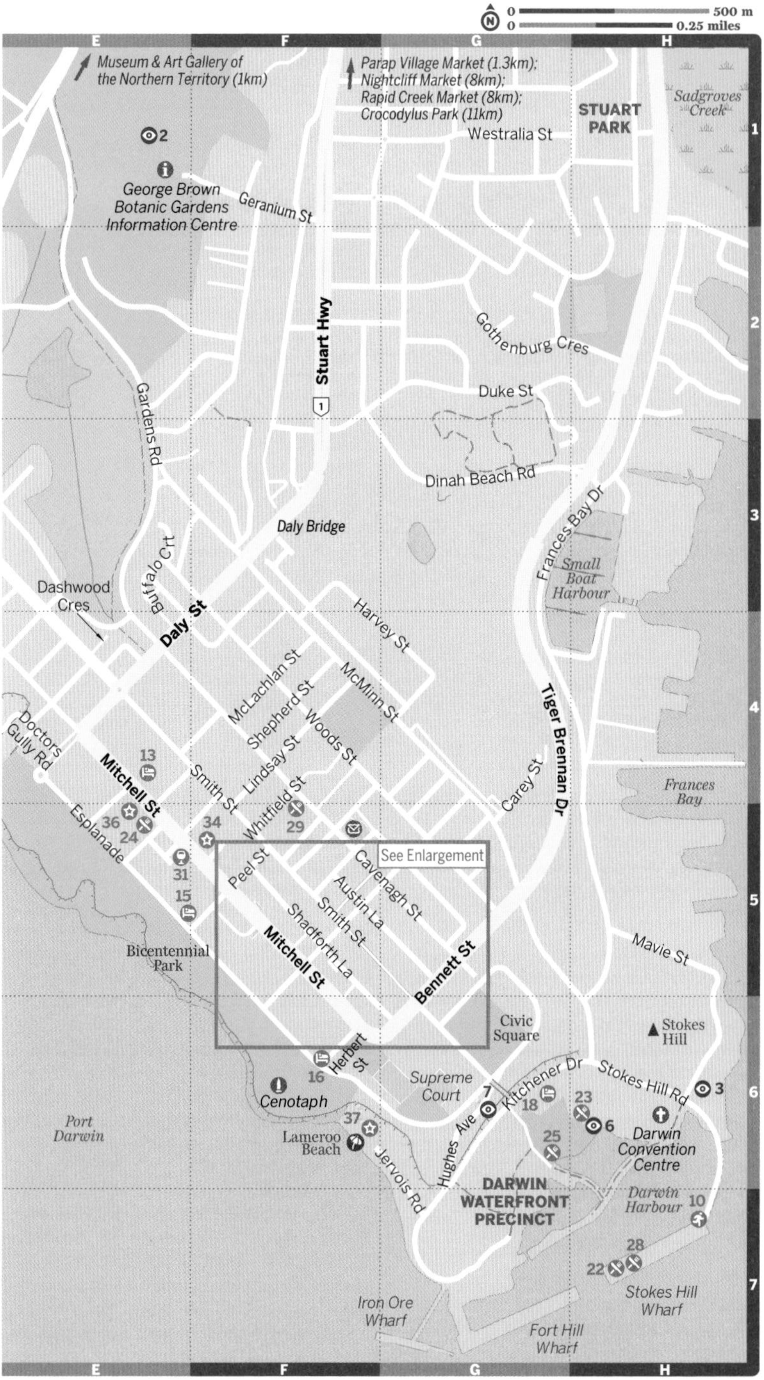
0 500 m
0 0.25 miles
E
F
G
H
1
2
3
4
5
6
7
Museum & Art Gallery of the Northern Territory (1km)
Parap Village Market (1.3km); Nightcliff Market (8km); Rapid Creek Market (8km); Crocodylus Park (11km)
STUART PARK
Sadgroves Creek
Westralia St
2
George Brown Botanic Gardens Information Centre
Geranium St
Stuart Hwy
1
Gothenburg Cres
Duke St
Gardens Rd
Dinah Beach Rd
Frances Bay Dr
Daly Bridge
Small Boat Harbour
Buffalo Crt
Dashwood Cres
Daly St
Harvey St
McLachlan St
McMinn St
Shepherd St
Woods St
Lindsay St
Tiger Brennan Dr
Doctors Gully Rd
Mitchell St
Smith St
Carey St
Frances Bay
13
Whitfield St
36
24
34
29
Esplanade
31
Peel St
See Enlargement
Cavenagh St
15
Austin La
Smith St
Shadforth La
Mitchell St
Bennett St
Mavie St
Bicentennial Park
Civic Square
Stokes Hill
Herbert St
16
Supreme Court
Kitchener Dr
Stokes Hill Rd
3
Cenotaph
7
18
23
6
Port Darwin
37
Hughes Ave
25
Darwin Convention Centre
Lameroo Beach
Jervois Rd
DARWIN WATERFRONT PRECINCT
Darwin Harbour
10
28
22
Stokes Hill Wharf
Iron Ore Wharf
Fort Hill Wharf

Darwin

Top Sights

1 Crocosaurus Cove A6

Sights

Burnett House .... (see 5)
Coral Reef By Night .... (see 3)
2 George Brown Botanic Gardens E1
3 Indo-Pacific Marine Exhibition H6
4 Mindil Beach Sunset Market D1
5 Myilly Point Heritage Precinct D2
6 Wave & Recreation Lagoons H6
7 WWII Oil-Storage Tunnels G6

Activities, Courses & Tours

8 Anniki Pearl Lugger Cruises B2
9 Darwin Day Tours A6
10 Sunset Sail H7

Sleeping

11 Chilli's A6
12 Darwin Central Hotel B6
13 Dingo Moon Lodge E4
14 Elan Soho Suites D5
Melaleuca on Mitchell .... (see 17)
15 Novotel Atrium E5
16 Palms City Resort F6
17 Value Inn B6
18 Vibe Hotel G6
19 Youth Shack A6

Eating

20 Char Restaurant A7
21 Coles B6
22 Crustaceans H7
23 Curve H6
24 Hanuman E5
25 Hot Tamale G6
26 Moorish Café C5
27 Roma Bar C6
28 Stokes Hill Wharf H7
29 Woolworths F5

Drinking & Nightlife

30 Deck Bar C7
31 Discovery & Lost Arc E5
32 Tap on Mitchell A6
33 Throb B5

Entertainment

34 Birch Carroll & Coyle F5
35 Brown's Mart C7
36 Darwin Entertainment Centre E5
37 Deckchair Cinema F6
38 Happy Yess C7

Shopping

39 Aboriginal Fine Arts Gallery B6
40 Mbantua Fine Art Gallery C7
41 NT General Store C5

multimillion-dollar redevelopment features a cruise-ship terminal, luxury hotels, boutique restaurants and shopping, the Sky Bridge, an elevated walkway and elevator at the south end of Smith St, and a Wave Lagoon.

Wave & Recreation Lagoons WATER PARK
(☎08-8985 6588; www.waterfront.nt.gov.au; Wave Lagoon adult/child $7/5; ⊙Wave Lagoon 10am-6pm) The hugely popular **Wave Lagoon** is a hit with locals and travellers alike. There are 10 different wave patterns produced (20 minutes on with a 10-minute rest in between) and there are lifeguards, a kiosk and a strip of lawn to bask on. Adjacent is the **Recreation Lagoon** with a sandy beach, lifeguards and stinger-filtered seawater (although the nets and filters are not guaranteed to be 100% effective).

WWII Oil-Storage Tunnels TUNNEL
☎08-8985 6322; www.darwintours.com.au/ww2tunnels; self-guided tour per person $7; ⊙9am-4pm May-Sep, to 1pm Oct-Apr) You can escape from the heat of the day and relive your Hitchcockian fantasies by walking through the WWII oil-storage tunnels. They were built in 1942 to store the navy's oil supplies (but never used); now they exhibit wartime photos.

Indo-Pacific Marine Exhibition AQUARIUM
(☎08-8981 1294; www.indopacificmarine.com.au; 29 Stokes Hill Rd; adult/child $24/10; ⊙10am-4pm Apr-Oct, call Nov-Mar) This excellent marine aquarium at the Waterfront Precinct gives you a close encounter with the denizens at the bottom of Darwin Harbour. Each small tank is a complete ecosystem, with only the occasional extra fish introduced as food for some of the predators, such as stonefish or the bizarre angler fish.

Also recommended here is the **Coral Reef by Night** (☎08-8981 1294; www.indopacificmarine.com.au; 29 Stokes Hill Rd; adult/child $120/60; ⊙6.30pm Wed, Fri & Sun), which consists of a tour of the aquarium, seafood dinner (on biodegradable plates, no less!) and an impressive show of fluorescing animals.

★ **Museum & Art Gallery of the Northern Territory** MUSEUM
(MAGNT; ☎08-8999 8264; www.magnt.net.au; 19 Conacher St, Fannie Bay; ⏱9am-5pm Mon-Fri, 10am-5pm Sat & Sun) FREE This superb museum and gallery boasts beautifully presented galleries of Top End–centric exhibits. The **Aboriginal art collection** is a highlight, with carvings from the Tiwi Islands, bark paintings from Arnhem Land and dot paintings from the desert. An entire room is devoted to **Cyclone Tracy**, in a display that graphically illustrates life before and after the 1974 disaster. You can stand in a darkened room and listen to the whirring sound of Tracy at full throttle – a sound you won't forget in a hurry.

The cavernous **Maritime Gallery** houses an assortment of weird and wonderful crafts from the nearby islands and Indonesia, as well as a pearling lugger and a Vietnamese refugee boat.

Pride of place among the stuffed animals undoubtedly goes to Sweetheart: a 5m-long, 780kg saltwater crocodile. It became a Top End personality after attacking several fishing dinghies on the Finniss River, south of Darwin.

The museum has a good bookshop, and the Cornucopia Cafe is a great lunch spot with views over the sea.

Crocodylus Park ZOO
(www.crocodyluspark.com.au; 815 McMillans Rd, Berrimah; adult/child $40/20; ⏱9am-5pm) Crocodylus Park showcases hundreds of crocs and a minizoo comprising lions, tigers and other big cats, spider monkeys, marmosets, cassowaries and large birds. Allow about two hours to look around the whole park, and you should time your visit with a **tour** (10am, noon, 2pm and 3.30pm), which includes a feeding demonstration. Croc-meat BBQ packs for sale!

The park is about 15km from the city centre. Take bus 5 from Darwin.

Activities

Beaches & Swimming

Darwin is no beach paradise – naturally enough the harbour has no surf – but along the convoluted coastline north of the city centre is a string of sandy beaches. The most popular are **Mindil** and **Vestey's** on Fannie Bay. Further north, a stretch of the 7km **Casuarina Beach** is an official nude beach. Darwin's swimming beaches tend to be far enough away from mangrove creeks to make the threat of meeting a crocodile very remote. A bigger problem is the deadly box jellyfish, which makes swimming decidedly unhealthy between October and March (and often before October and until May). You can swim year-round without fear of stingers in the western part of **Lake Alexander**, an easy cycle from the centre at **East Point** (⏱mangrove boardwalk 8am-6pm), and at the very popular Wave & Recreation Lagoons (p78), the centrepiece of the Darwin Wharf Precinct. At the Recreation Lagoon, filtered seawater and nets provide a natural seawater swim.

Tours

There are dozens of tours in and around Darwin, and lots of combinations covering Kakadu, Arnhem Land, Litchfield and further afield.

Batji Indigenous Waterfront Walking Tour CULTURAL TOUR
(☎0416 731 353; www.batjitours.com.au; adult/child $70/free; ⏱10am Wed & Fri) An excellent two-hour walking tour along the Esplanade run by the Larrakia people of Darwin. You will learn about the local wildlife, discover Lameroo beach and gain insight into places of cultural significance to the Larrakia people.

Darwin Explorer BUS TOUR
(☎0416 140 903; http://theaustralianexplorer.com.au/darwin-explorer.html; 24hr ticket adult/child $35/20) Open-top bus tours that explore Darwin's major sights; hop on/hop off with either a 24-hour or 48-hour ticket. Departs every 30 minutes from the tourist information centre.

Tour Tub BUS TOUR
(☎08-8985 6322; www.tourtub.com.au; adult/child $100/60) Offering five-hour guided, minibus tours around Darwin's big-ticket sights; price includes admission charges to attractions such as Defence of Darwin Experience.

Sea Darwin ECOTOUR
(☎1300 065 022; www.seadarwin.com; tours adult/child from $35/20) One-, two- or three-hour eco tours around the city and Darwin Harbour, checking out mangroves, a crocodile trap, a shipwreck and (if you're lucky) dugongs and dolphins.

Darwin Day Tours TOUR
(☎1300 721 365; www.darwindaytours.com.au; afternoon city tours adult/child $75/38) Runs an afternoon city tour that takes in all the

major attractions, including Stokes Hill Wharf, the Museum & Art Gallery and East Point Reserve. Can be linked with a 'sunset fish 'n' chips harbour cruise' ($55/40).

Tiwi Tours CULTURAL TOUR
(☎1300 721 365; www.aussieadventures.com.au; adult/child incl flights $550/410) Small-group cultural tours out to the nearby Tiwi Islands with Indigenous guides (adult/child including flights $550/410). Kakadu and Litchfield tours also available through the company's other brands: Darwin Day Tours and Aussie Adventure.

Northern Territory Indigenous Tours CULTURAL TOUR
(☎1300 921 188; www.ntitours.com.au; adult/child $249/124) Upmarket Indigenous tours to Litchfield National Park.

Sacred Earth Safaris OUTDOORS
(☎08-8555 3838; www.sacredearthsafaris.com.au) Multiday, small-group 4WD camping tours around Kakadu, Katherine and the Kimberley. Two-day Kakadu tour starts at $850; the five-day Top End National Parks Safari is $2600.

Kakadu Dreams TOUR
(☎1800 813 266; www.kakadudreams.com.au) Backpacker day tours to Litchfield ($119), and boisterous two-/three-day trips to Kakadu ($400/535).

Wallaroo Tours TOUR
(☎08-8981 6670; www.wallarootours.com; tours $160) Small-group tours to Litchfield National Park.

Harbour Cruises

Between April and October there are plenty of boats based at the Cullen Bay Marina and Stokes Hill Wharf to take you on a cruise of the harbour.

Anniki Pearl Lugger Cruises SAILING
(☎0428 414 000; www.australianharbourcruises.com.au; tours adult/child $70/50) Three-hour sunset cruises on this historical pearling lugger depart from Cullen Bay Marina and include sparkling wine and nibbles. You might recognise the ship from the film *Australia*.

Sunset Sail SAILING
(☎0408 795 567; www.sailnt.com.au; tours adult/child $70/45) This three-hour afternoon cruise aboard the catamaran *Daymirri 2* departs from Stokes Hill Wharf. Refreshments are included but BYO alcohol.

Festivals & Events

WordStorm LITERATURE
(www.wordstorm.org.au) The biannual NT Writers' Festival event in May (even-numbered years) includes song, storytelling, visual-art collaboration, theatre, performance poetry, history, biography, poetry and fiction.

Darwin Blues Festival MUSIC
In late June the Darwin Botanic Gardens charge up with electrifying live blues. Much beer and bending of guitar strings.

Beer Can Regatta CULTURAL
(www.beercanregatta.org.au) An utterly insane and typically Territorian festival that features races for boats made out of beer cans. It takes place at Mindil Beach in July and is a good, fun day.

Darwin Aboriginal Art Fair ART
(www.darwinaboriginalartfair.com.au) Held at the Darwin Convention Centre, this three-day August festival showcases Indigenous art from communities throughout the Northern Territory.

Darwin Festival ART
(www.darwinfestival.org.au) This mainly outdoor arts and culture festival celebrates music, theatre, visual art, dance and cabaret and runs for 18 days in August. Festivities are centred in the large park next to Civic Sq, off Harry Chan Ave.

Sleeping

Darwin has a good range of accommodation, most of it handy to the CBD, but finding a bed in the peak May to September period can be difficult at short notice – book ahead, at least for the first night. Accommodation prices vary greatly with the season and demand; expect big discounts between November and March, especially for midrange and top-end accommodation.

Melaleuca on Mitchell HOSTEL $
(☎1300 723 437; www.momdarwin.com.au; 52 Mitchell St; dm $32, d with/without bathroom $115/95; ❄@🛜🏊) If you stay here take note – 24-hour check-in and it's plonked right in the action on Mitchell St. So, sleeping... maybe not. Partying? Oh yes! The highlight is the rooftop island bar and pool area overlooking Mitchell St – complete with waterfall spa and big-screen TV. Party heaven! This modern hostel is immaculate with great facilities and it's very secure. The 3rd floor is female only.

RICHARD I'ANSON/GETTY IMAGES ©

Wave Lagoon (p78), Darwin Waterfront Precinct

Dingo Moon Lodge HOSTEL $
(☎08-8941 3444; www.dingomoonlodge.com; 88 Mitchell St; incl breakfast dm $32-38, d & tw $105; ❄@🛜≋) Howl at the moon at the Dingo. This fun, laid-back hostel is slightly removed from the party scene, although everything is still at your doorstep. It's a two-building affair with 65 beds – big enough to be sociable but not rowdy. Cleanliness and service tend to fluctuate. A highlight is the pool, sparkling underneath a massive frangipani tree.

Chilli's HOSTEL $
(☎1800 351 313, 08-8980 5800; www.chillis.com.au; 69a Mitchell St; dm $34, tw & d without bathroom $100; ❄@🛜) Friendly Chilli's is a funky place with a small sun deck and spa (use the pool next door). There's also a pool table and a breezy kitchen/meals terrace overlooking Mitchell St. Rooms are compact but clean. There are nice touches to this place, such as pots with scented herbs hanging from the roof of the balcony.

Youth Shack HOSTEL $
(☎1300 793 302; www.youthshack.com.au; 69 Mitchell St; dm $34, tw & d without bathroom $90; ≋) At one end of the Transit Centre, this popular hostel has a large open kitchen and meals area overlooking a pool big enough to actually swim in. The bar here is very popular and at times raucous. Rooms are a little tired but clean, and the staff are consistently praised for being friendly and helpful. The tour desk here has a great reputation.

Darwin Central Hotel HOTEL $$
(☎08-8944 9000, 1300 364 263; www.darwincentral.com.au; 21 Knuckey St; d from $180; P❄@🛜≋🐾) Right in the centre of town, this plush independent hotel oozes contemporary style and impeccable facilities. There are a range of stylish rooms with excellent accessibility for disabled travellers. Rack rates are steep, but internet, weekend and three-night-stay discounts make it great value. The excellent breakfast caps things off nicely.

Value Inn HOTEL $$
(☎08-8981 4733; www.valueinn.com.au; 50 Mitchell St; d from $140; P❄≋) A great option right in the thick of the Mitchell St action but (mostly) quiet and comfortable. Value Inn lives up to its name, especially out of season. En suite rooms are small but sleep up to three and have fridge and TV.

Palms City Resort RESORT $$
(☎1800 829 211, 08-8982 9200; http://palmscityresort.com; 64 The Esplanade; d motel/villas $230/280; P❄🛜≋) Consistently receiving the thumbs up from travellers, this centrally located resort is fringed by palm-filled gardens. If you covet a microwave and have space cravings, the superior motel rooms are worth a bit extra, while the Asian-influenced, hexagonal villas with outdoor spas are utterly indulgent. Butterflies and dragonflies drift between bougainvillea in the knockout gardens.

Vibe Hotel
HOTEL $$$

(☑08-8982 9998; www.tfehotels.com/brands/vibe-hotels/vibe-hotel-darwin-waterfront; 7 Kitchener Dr; r $260-310; P✳@🛜🏊) You're in for an upmarket stay at this professional set-up with friendly staff and a great location at the Darwin Waterfront Precinct. Room prices creep upwards with more bed space and water views. The Wave Lagoon is right next door if the shady swimming pool is too placid for you.

Elan Soho Suites
HOTEL, APARTMENTS $$$

(☑08-8981 0888; www.elansohosuites.com; 31 Woods St; r $220, 1-/2-bedroom apt $270/310; P✳🛜🏊) This innovative newcomer was still in the midst of major renovations when we dropped in, but had just started to accept guests. Room prices (at least initially, while the place gets established) promise to be great value. Views are stunning, facilities first-rate; you can even check-in online, and unlock your room door via your mobile phone. Its restaurant 'Seoul Food' brings Korean cooking to Darwin.

Novotel Atrium
HOTEL $$$

(☑08-8941 0755; www.novotel.com; 100 The Esplanade; d from $350, 2-bedroom apt from $470; P✳@🛜🏊) Yes, it's a chain hotel, but this one, with to-die-for ocean views, stands out from the crowd. Stylistic standards are above the norm: subtle lighting, fresh flowers and interesting Indigenous art. Breathe the sea air on your balcony or descend into the kidney-shaped swimming pool, one of the best-looking puddles in Darwin. Breakfasts are a highlight.

🍴 Eating

Darwin is the glistening pearl in the Territory's dining scene. Eateries make the most of the tropical ambience with alfresco seating, and the quality and diversity of produce top anywhere else in the Territory.

There are two large supermarkets in downtown Darwin: **Coles** (55-59 Mitchell St, Mitchell Centre; ⊘24hr) and **Woolworths** (cnr Cavenagh & Whitfield Sts; ⊘6am-10pm).

Roma Bar
CAFE $

(☑08-8981 6729; www.romabar.com.au; 9-11 Cavenagh St; mains $8-15; ⊘7am-4pm Mon-Fri, 8am-2pm Sat, 8am-1pm Sun; 🛜) Roma is a local institution and the most reliable place for quality coffee in Darwin. It's a meeting place for lefties, literati and travellers. It's well away from the craziness of Mitchell St, with free wi-fi and fresh juices, and you can get anything from muesli and eggs Benedict for breakfast to excellent toasted focaccia and even fish curry for lunch.

Stokes Hill Wharf
SEAFOOD, FAST FOOD $$

(Stokes Hill Wharf; mains $10-20; ⊘from 11am) Squatting on the end of Stokes Hill Wharf is a hectic food centre with a dozen food counters and outdoor tables lined up along the pier. It's a pumping place for some fish and chips, oysters, a stir-fry, a laksa or a cold sunset beer.

Didgeridoos for sale, Mindil Beach Sunset Market (p84)

Crustaceans SEAFOOD $$
(☎ 08-8981 8658; www.crustaceans.net.au; Stokes Hill Wharf; mains $18-40; ⏲ from 5.30pm; 👪) This casual, licensed restaurant features fresh fish, bugs, lobster, oysters, even crocodile, as well as succulent steaks. It's all about the location, perched right at the end of Stokes Hill Wharf with sunset views over Frances Bay. The cold beer and a first-rate wine list seal the deal.

Hot Tamale MEXICAN $$
(☎ 08-8981 5471; www.hottamale.net.au; Bldg 3, 19 Kitchener Dr; mains $20-25; ⏲ noon-9pm) With drink specials aplenty and a fun, laid-back attitude, this place is recommended as much for the atmosphere and brilliant waterfront location as for the delicious Mexican food. Tacos, burritos and nachos galore.

Curve CAFE $$
(☎ 08-8982 9709; 7 Kitchener Dr; mains $22-35; ⏲ 6am-9pm; 👪) Spacious and clean inside and with comfy seating out the front to catch the breeze, this all-rounder is good for a bite any time of the day. Lunch is a good deal: a burger or panini with a beer or glass of wine is $18. In the evening tuck into pan-seared Cajun tuna. It's opposite the Wave Lagoon – handy for families needing extra shade or something to fuel up on.

Moorish Café MIDDLE EASTERN $$$
(☎ 08-8981 0010; www.moorishcafe.com.au; 37 Knuckey St; tapas $7-11, mains $33; ⏲ 9am-2.30pm & 6-10pm Tue-Fri, 9am-10pm Sat) Seductive aromas emanate from this divine terracotta-tiled cafe fusing North African, Mediterranean and Middle Eastern delights. The tapas can be a bit hit-and-miss but dishes such as the pork belly with chilli-chocolate sauce and Berber spiced kangaroo are tasty and reliable. It's a lovely dining experience, especially with a table overlooking the street.

Hanuman INDIAN, THAI $$$
(☎ 08-8941 3500; www.hanuman.com.au; 93 Mitchell St; mains $19-38; ⏲ noon-2.30pm, dinner from 6pm; 🌿) Ask most locals about fine dining in Darwin and they'll usually mention Hanuman. It's sophisticated but not stuffy. Enticing aromas of innovative Indian and Thai Nonya dishes waft from the kitchen to the stylish open dining room and deck. The menu is broad, with exotic vegetarian choices and banquets also available.

Char Restaurant STEAK $$$
(☎ 08-8981 4544; www.charrestaurant.com.au; cnr The Esplanade & Knuckey St; mains $30-60; ⏲ noon-3pm Wed-Fri, 6-11pm daily) Housed in the grounds of the historic Admiralty House is Char, a carnivore's paradise. The speciality here is chargrilled steaks – aged, grain-fed and cooked to perfection – but there's also a range of clever seafood creations such as banana prawn and crab tian, with avocado purée and *tobiko* caviar.

LOCAL KNOWLEDGE

PARAP VILLAGE MARKET

Parap Village is a foodie's heaven with several good restaurants, bars and cafes as well as the highly recommended deli **Parap Fine Foods** (☎ 08-8981 8597; www.parapfinefoods.com; 40 Parap Rd, Parap; ⏲ 8am-6.30pm Mon-Fri, to 6pm Sat, 9am-1pm Sun). However, it's the Saturday morning **markets** (p84) that attract locals like bees to honey. It's got a relaxed vibe as breakfast merges into brunch and then lunch. Between visits to the takeaway food stalls (most serving spicy Southeast Asian snacks) shoppers stock up on tropical fruit and vegetables – all you need to make your own laksa or rendang. The produce is local so you know it's fresh.

🍷 Drinking & Nightlife

Drinking is big business in tropical Darwin (cold beer and humidity have a symbiotic relationship), and the city has dozens of pubs and terrace bars that make the most of balmy evenings. Virtually all bars double as restaurants, especially along Mitchell St – a frenzied row of booze rooms full of travellers, all within stumbling distance of one another.

Tap on Mitchell BAR
(www.thetap.com.au; 51 Mitchell St) One of the busiest and best of the Mitchell St terrace bars, the Tap is always buzzing and there are inexpensive meals (nachos, burgers, calamari) to complement a great range of beer and wine.

Beachfront Hotel PUB
(☎ 08-8985 3000; 342 Casuarina Dr, Rapid Creek) Close to the border of Nightcliff, this rollicking pub attracts a local crowd and often has bands. A spot out on the breezy front deck with a cold drink is ideal.

Deck Bar BAR
(www.thedeckbar.com.au; 22 Mitchell St) At the nonpartying parliamentary end of Mitchell

DARWIN'S MAGICAL MARKETS

Mindil Beach Sunset Market (www.mindil.com.au; off Gilruth Ave; ⏲5-10pm Thu, 4-9pm Sun May-Oct) Food is the main attraction here – from Thai, Sri Lankan, Indian, Chinese and Malaysian to Brazilian, Greek, Portuguese and more – all at around \$6 to \$12 a serve. But that's only half the fun – arts and crafts stalls bulge with handmade jewellery, fabulous rainbow tie-dyed clothes, Aboriginal artefacts, and wares from Indonesia and Thailand. Mindil Beach is about 2km from Darwin's city centre; an easy walk or hop on buses 4 or 6 which go past the market area.

As the sun heads towards the horizon, half of Darwin descends on the market, with tables, chairs, rugs, grog and kids in tow. Peruse and promenade, stop for a pummelling massage or to listen to rhythmic live music. Don't miss a flaming satay stick from Bobby's brazier. Top it off with fresh fruit salad, decadent cakes or luscious crêpes.

Similar stalls (you'll recognise many of the stallholders) can be found at various suburban markets from Friday to Sunday.

Parap Village Market (www.parapvillage.com.au; Parap Shopping Village, Parap Rd, Parap; ⏲8am-2pm Sat) This compact, crowded, food-focused market is a local favourite. There's the full gamut of Southeast Asian cuisine, as well as plenty of ingredients to cook up your own tropical storm.

Rapid Creek Market (www.rapidcreekshoppingcentre.com.au; 48 Trower Rd, Rapid Creek; ⏲6.30am-1.30pm Sun) Darwin's oldest market is an Asian marketplace, with a tremendous range of tropical fruit and vegetables mingled with a heady mixture of spices and swirling satay smoke.

Nightcliff Market (www.nightcliffmarkets.com.au; Pavonia Way, Nightcliff; ⏲6am-2pm Sun) A popular community market north of the city in the Nightcliff Shopping Centre. You'll find lots of secondhand goods and designer clothing.

St, the Deck Bar still manages to get lively with happy hours, pub trivia and regular live music. Blurring the line between indoors and outdoors brilliantly, the namesake deck is perfect for people-watching.

Discovery & Lost Arc CLUB
(www.discoverydarwin.com.au; 89 Mitchell St) Discovery is Darwin's biggest nightclub and dance venue, with three levels featuring hip-hop, techno and house, bars, private booths, karaoke, an elevated dance floor and plenty of partygoers. The Lost Arc is the classy chill-out bar opening on to Mitchell St, which starts to thaw after about 10pm.

☆ Entertainment

Darwin's balmy nights invite a bit of late-night exploration and while there are only a handful of nightclubs, you'll find something on every night of the week. There's also a thriving arts and entertainment scene: theatre, film and concerts.

Off the Leash (www.offtheleash.net.au) magazine lists events happening around town, as does **Darwin Community Arts** (www.darwincommunityarts.org.au). Keep an eye out for bills posted on noticeboards and telegraph poles that advertise dance and full-moon parties.

Just about every pub/bar in town puts on some form of live music, mostly on Friday and Saturday nights, and sometimes filling the midweek void with karaoke and DJs.

Throb CLUB
(64 Smith St; ⏲11pm-4am Fri & Sat) Darwin's premier gay- and lesbian-friendly nightclub and cocktail bar, Throb attracts partygoers of all genders and persuasions for its hot DJs and cool atmosphere. Hosts drag shows and touring live acts. Don't miss the Batman & Throbbin' show on Friday.

★ **Deckchair Cinema** CINEMA
(☎08-8981 0700; www.deckchaircinema.com; Jervois Rd, Waterfront Precinct; adult/child \$16/8; ⏲box office from 6.30pm Apr-Nov) During the Dry, the Darwin Film Society runs this fabulous outdoor cinema below the southern end of the Esplanade. Watch a movie under the stars while reclining in a deckchair. There's a licensed bar serving food or you can bring a picnic (no BYO alcohol). There are usually double features on Friday and Saturday nights (adult/child \$24/12).

Birch Carroll & Coyle CINEMA
(☎08-8981 5999; www.eventcinemas.com.au; 76 Mitchell St; adult/child $19/14.50) Darwin's mainstream cinema complex, screening the latest-release films across five theatres. Head down on Tropical Tuesday for $12.50 entry.

Darwin Entertainment Centre ARTS CENTRE
(☎08-8980 3333; www.darwinentertainment.com.au; 93 Mitchell St; ⏲box office 10am-5.30pm Mon-Fri & 1hr prior to shows) Darwin's main community arts venue houses the Playhouse and Studio Theatres, and hosts events from fashion-award nights to plays, rock operas, comedies and concerts.

Brown's Mart PERFORMING ARTS
(☎08-8981 5522; www.brownsmart.com.au; 12 Smith St) This historic venue (a former mining exchange) features live theatre performances, music and short films.

Happy Yess LIVE MUSIC
(happyyess.tumblr.com; 12 Smith St, Brown's Mart) This venue is Darwin's leading place for live music. It's run by musicians so you won't hear cover bands in here. Original, sometimes weird, always fun.

Shopping

You don't have to walk far along the Smith St Mall to find a souvenir shop selling lousy NT souvenirs: tea towels, T-shirts, stubbie holders and cane-toad coin purses (most of it made in China). Also in oversupply are outlets selling Aboriginal arts and crafts (be informed about reliable operators; see p67). Darwin's fabulous markets sell unique handcrafted items such as seed-pod hats, shell jewellery, kites, clothing and original photos.

NT General Store OUTDOOR EQUIPMENT
(☎08-8981 8242; www.thentgeneralstore.com.au; 42 Cavenagh St; ⏲8.30am-5.30pm Mon-Wed, to 6pm Thu & Fri, to 1pm Sat) This casual, corrugated-iron warehouse has shelves piled high with camping and bushwalking gear, as well as a range of maps.

Aboriginal Fine Arts Gallery ARTS
(www.aaia.com.au; 1st fl, cnr Mitchell & Knuckey Sts; ⏲9am-5pm) Displays and sells art from Arnhem Land and the central desert region.

Mbantua Fine Art Gallery ARTS
(☎08-8941 6611; www.mbantua.com.au; 2/30 Smith St Mall; ⏲9am-5pm Mon-Sat) Vivid Utopian designs painted on everything from canvases to ceramics.

Information

EMERGENCY

AANT Roadside Assistance (☎13 11 11; www.aant.com.au) Roadside assistance.

Ambulance (☎000) For emergencies.

Fire (☎000; www.nt.gov.au/pfes)

Poisons Information Centre (☎13 11 26; ⏲24hr) Advice on poisons, bites and stings.

Police (☎000; www.nt.gov.au/pfes) For local police service.

INTERNET ACCESS

Most accommodation in Darwin provides some form of internet access, and there is free wi-fi available in Smith St Mall.

Northern Territory Library (☎1800 019 155; www.ntl.nt.gov.au; Parliament House, Mitchell St; ⏲10am-5pm Mon-Fri, 1-5pm Sat & Sun; wi-fi) Book ahead for free access. Wi-fi also available.

MEDICAL SERVICES

Royal Darwin Hospital (☎08-8920 6011; www.health.nt.gov.au; Rocklands Dr, Tiwi; ⏲24hr) Accident and emergency.

MONEY

There are 24-hour ATMs dotted around the city centre, and exchange bureaux on Mitchell St.

POST

General Post Office (☎13 13 18; www.auspost.com.au; 48 Cavenagh St; ⏲9am-5pm Mon-Fri, to 12.30pm Sat) Efficient poste restante.

TOURIST INFORMATION

Tourism Top End (☎1300 138 886, 08-8980 6000; www.tourismtopend.com.au; cnr Smith & Bennett Sts; ⏲8.30am-5pm Mon-Fri, 9am-3pm Sat & Sun) Helpful office with hundreds of brochures; books tours and accommodation.

STRETCH YOUR LEGS DARWIN

Start/Finish: Crocosaurus Cove

Distance: 8.5km

Duration: 90 minutes

Darwin can get very humid – start early, stick to the shady side of the street and keep close to the water. Follow these rules and you'll find an engaging city that's proud of its place on Australia's northern frontier.

Take this walk on Trip

2

Crocosaurus Cove

There's no more appropriate way to begin in the Top End than with the anything-but-humble croc. Right in the middle of Mitchell St, **Crocosaurus Cove** (☎08-8981 7522; www.crocosauruscove.com; 58 Mitchell St; adult/child $32/20; ⌚9am-6pm, last admission 5pm) is as close as you'll ever want to get to these amazing creatures. Six of the largest crocs in captivity can be seen in state-of-the-art aquariums and pools. You can be lowered right into a pool with the crocs in the transparent Cage of Death (one/two people $160/240).

The Walk » From Crocosaurus Cove, walk 150m southeast along Mitchell St. The next stop is on your left, on the corner with Knuckey St. Along the way, Tap on Mitchell is one of the busiest and best of the area's terrace bars: there are inexpensive meals to complement a great range of beers and wine.

Aboriginal Fine Arts Gallery

Darwin is an important centre for Indigenous art from artists across the Top End, and this excellent **gallery** (www.aaia.com.au; 1st fl, cnr Mitchell & Knuckey Sts; ⌚9am-5pm) displays and sells art from Arnhem Land and the central desert region.

The Walk » Take Knuckey St, heading towards the Esplanade. Lyons Cottage is to your right.

Lyons Cottage

Built in 1925, **Lyons Cottage** (cnr Esplanade & Knuckey St) was Darwin's first stone residence, formerly housing executives from the British Australian Telegraph Company (which laid a submarine cable between Australia and Java). It's one of Darwin's most attractive downtown structures (not many buildings last that long in the tropical heat and humidity).

The Walk » Cross over the Esplanade to Bicentennial Park.

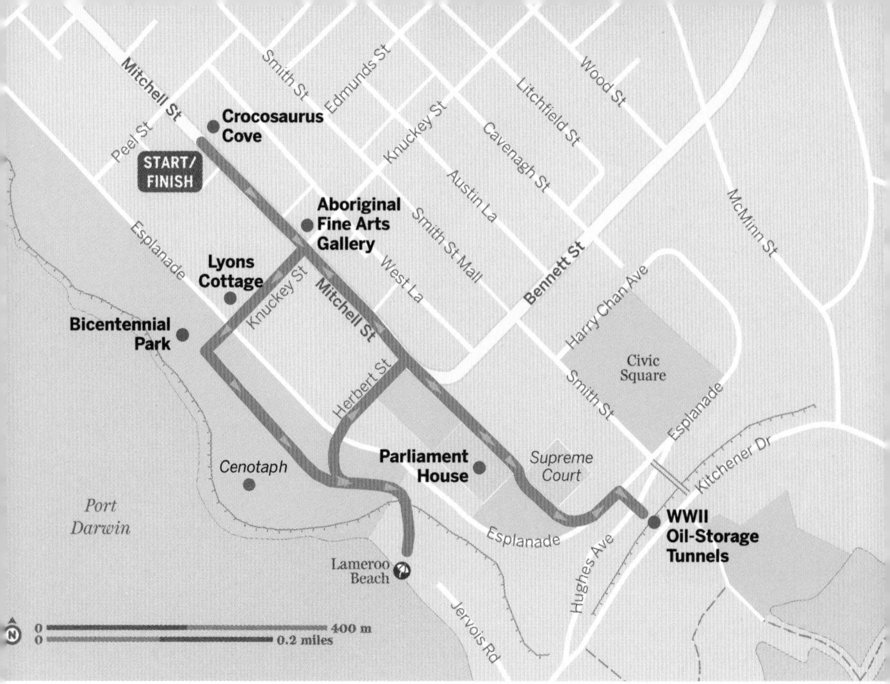

Bicentennial Park

Running the length of Darwin's waterfront **Bicentennial Park** (The Esplanade) is shaded by tropical trees and is an excellent place to stroll. Lameroo Beach is a sheltered cove that was popular in the '20s when it housed the saltwater baths, and traditionally a Larrakia camp area.

The Walk » Stroll through the park to the Cenotaph and down to Lameroo Beach. Then, walk back through the park, cross the Esplanade and walk up Herbert St. Turn right into Mitchell St. Where Mitchell St ends (or loops around to the left), Parliament House lies straight ahead.

Parliament House

At the southern end of Mitchell St is the elegantly box-like **Parliament House** (☎08-8946 1512; www.nt.gov.au/lant; Mitchell St; ⌚8am-4.30pm), which opened in 1994. Reminiscent of Southeast Asian colonial architecture, it's designed to withstand Darwin's monsoonal climate. Attend one of the tours exploring the cavernous interior on Saturday at 9am and 11am (no booking required).

The Walk » Pass the Supreme Court, and the WWII Oil-Storage Tunnels are accessible via a walkway from the Esplanade to Kitchener Dr.

WWII Oil-Storage Tunnels

You can escape from the heat of the day and relive your Hitchcockian fantasies by walking through the **WWII Oil-Storage Tunnels** (☎08-8985 6322; www.darwintours.com.au/ww2tunnels; self-guided tour per person $7; ⌚9am-4pm May-Sep, to 1pm Oct-Apr). They were built in 1942 to store the navy's oil supplies (but never used); now they exhibit wartime photos.

The Walk » Retrace your steps back to Parliament House and then continue along Mitchell St back to Crocosaurus Cove.

South to Adelaide

Along the Stuart Hwy, towns such as Coober Pedy and Port Augusta emerge from the heat haze. This is no country for the faint-hearted: it's waterless, flyblown and dizzyingly hot. No wonder the opal miners in Coober Pedy live underground!

Coober Pedy

POP 3500

Coming into cosmopolitan Coober Pedy (there are 44 nationalities represented here!) the dry, barren desert suddenly becomes riddled with holes and adjunct piles of dirt – reputedly more than a million around the township. The reason for all this rabid digging is opals. Discovered here 100 years ago, these gemstones have made this small town a mining mecca.

The surrounding desert is jaw-droppingly desolate, a fact not overlooked by international filmmakers who've come here to shoot end-of-the-world epics like *Mad Max III, Red Planet, Ground Zero, Pitch Black* and the slightly more believable *Adventures of Priscilla, Queen of the Desert.*

Sights

Big Winch SCULPTURE, VIEWPOINT

You can't miss the Big Winch, from which there are sweeping views over Coober Pedy. An optimistic 'if' painted on the side of the big bucket sums up the town's spirit.

Spaceship SCULPTURE

Check out this amazing leftover prop from the film *Pitch Black,* which has crash-landed on Hutchison St.

Tom's Working Opal Mine MINE

(www.tomsworkingopalmine.com; Lot 1993, Stuart Hwy; tours adult/child/family $25/10/55; 8am-5pm) The best place to check out a working excavation is Tom's, 2km southwest of town: miners continue their search for the big vein; visitors noodle for small fortunes. Self-guided tours run from 8am to 5pm and cost $10 per adult, $5 per child.

Old Timers Mine MUSEUM

(www.oldtimersmine.com; 1 Crowders Gully Rd; self-guided tours adult/child/family $15/5/40; 9am-5.30pm) This interesting warren of tunnels was mined in 1916, and then hidden by the miners. The mine was rediscovered when excavations for a dugout home punched through into the labyrinth of tunnels. As well as the great self-guided tunnel tours, there's a museum, a re-created 1920s underground home, and free mining-equipment demos daily (9.30am, 1.30pm and 3.30pm).

Dugout Homes & Churches

Even when it's face-meltingly hot here in summer, subterranean temperatures never exceed 23°C – no air-con required for underground houses! The same goes for churches (miners are big on faith and hope).

Faye's Underground Home UNDERGROUND

(08-8672 5029; www.cooberpedy.sa.gov.au; Old Water Tank Rd; adult/child $5/1.50; 8am-5pm Mon-Sat Mar-Oct) Faye's was hand dug by three women in the 1960s. It's a little flowery, but the living-room swimming pool is a winner!

Serbian Orthodox Church CHURCH
(☎08-8672 3048; Saint Elijah Dr, off Flinders St; admission $5; ⏲24hr) This is the town's largest and most impressive underground church, with intricate rock-wall carvings and a gorgeous vaulted ceiling. It's about 3km south of town.

Catholic Church of St Peter & St Paul CHURCH
(cnr Halliday Pl & Hutchison St; ⏲10am-4pm daily, Mass 10am Sun) FREE Coober Pedy's first church still has a sweet appeal, with statue-filled nooks and hushed classical music.

Tours

Arid Areas Tours DRIVING TOUR
(☎08-8672 3008; www.aridareastours.com; 2-/4-/6hr tours per 2 people from $120/240/420) Offers 4WD tours around town, extending to the Painted Desert and the Breakaways.

Desert Cave Tours TOUR
(☎1800 088 521, 08-8672 5688; www.desertcave.com.au; 4hr tours per adult/child $98/49) A convenient highlight tour taking in the town, the Dog Fence, the Breakaways and Moon Plain. Also on offer are four-hour 'Down 'N' Dirty' opal-digging tours (adult/child $110/55).

Mail Run Tour DRIVING TOUR
(☎08-8672 5226, 1800 069 911; www.mailruntour.com; tours per person $195) Coober Pedy–based full-day mail-run tours through the desert and along the Oodnadatta Track to Oodnadatta and William Creek return.

Opal Air SCENIC FLIGHTS
(☎08-8670 7997; www.opalair.com.au; flights per person from $470) Half-day scenic flights from Coober Pedy winging over Lake Eyre, William Creek and the Painted Desert.

Sleeping

Riba's CAMPGROUND $
(☎08-8672 5614; www.camp-underground.com.au; Lot 1811 William Creek Rd; underground sites $30, above-ground unpowered/powered sites $20/28, s & d $66; 📶) Around 5km from town, Riba's offers the unique option of underground camping! Extras include an underground TV lounge, cell-like underground budget rooms and a nightly opal-mine tour (adult $24; free for underground and unpowered-site campers, discounted for other guests).

ANDREW WATSON/GETTY IMAGES ©

Bar in Faye's Underground Home, Coober Pedy

Coober Pedy

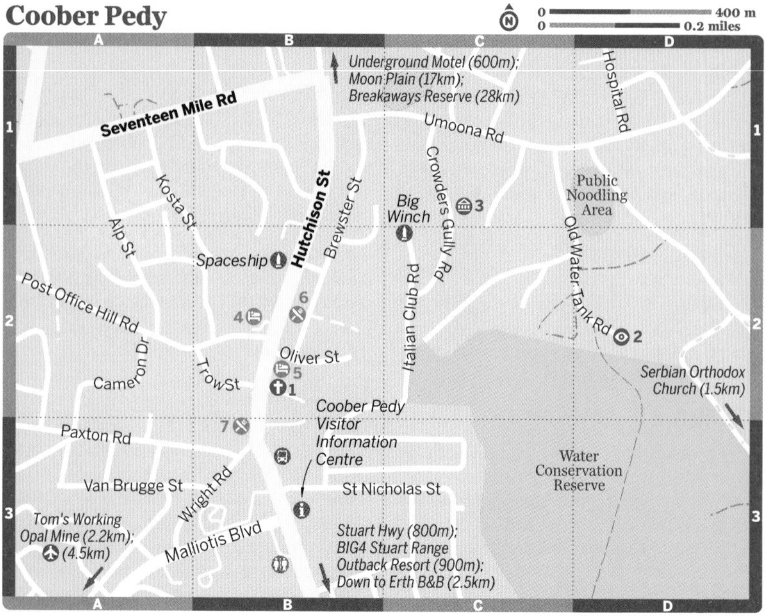

Coober Pedy

Sights

1 Catholic Church of St Peter & St Paul B2
2 Faye's Underground Home D2
3 Old Timers Mine C1

Sleeping

4 Desert Cave Hotel B2
5 Radeka Downunder B2

Eating

6 John's Pizza Bar & Restaurant B2
7 Tom & Mary's Greek Taverna B3
Umberto's ..... (see 4)

BIG4 Stuart Range Outback Resort CARAVAN PARK $
(☎08-8672 5179; www.stuartrangeoutbackresort.com.au; Yanikas Dr; unpowered/powered sites $27/34, d from $99, 1-/2-bedroom apt $170/255; ❄📶🏊) Spending up big on renovating their units and extensive landscaping (oh look – olive trees!), Stuart Range is probably the best traditional (ie above-ground!) caravan park around town. The pool was being renovated when we visited: make sure it's full before you dive in. Tours also available.

Radeka Downunder HOSTEL $
(☎08-8672 5223; www.radekadownunder.com.au; 1 Oliver St; dm/d/tr/q $35/85/120/155, motel units d/tr/f $130/165/200; @📶) The owners started excavating this place in 1960: they haven't found much opal, but they sure have an interesting backpackers! On multiple levels extending 6.5m underground are budget beds, plus passable individual rooms and motel units. There's also a shared kitchen/bar, barbecue, laundry, tours and airport transfers. Getting some mixed reviews of late.

★ **Down to Erth B&B** B&B $$
(☎08-8672 5762; www.downtoerth.com.au; Lot 1785 Monument Rd; d incl breakfast $165, extra person $25; 📶🏊) A real dugout gem about 3km from town: your own subterranean two-bedroom bunker (sleeps five – perfect for a family) with a kitchen-lounge area, a shady plunge pool for cooling off after a day exploring the Earth, wood-fuelled BBQ and complimentary chocolates.

Desert Cave Hotel HOTEL $$
(☎08-8672 5688; www.desertcave.com.au; Lot 1 Hutchison St; d/tr from $170/200, extra person $35; ❄@📶🏊) Top of the CP price tree, the Desert Cave brings a much-needed shot of desert luxury – plus a beaut pool, a daytime

cafe, airport transfers and the excellent **Umberto's** (08-8672 5688; www.desertcave.com.au; Lot 1 Hutchison St; mains $28-38; 6-9pm) restaurant. Staff are supercourteous and there are tours on offer. Above-ground rooms also available (huge, but there are more soulful places to stay in town).

Underground Motel MOTEL $$
(08-8672 5324; www.theunderground-motel.com.au; Catacomb Rd; standard s/d/f $110/125/157, ste $125/135/182;) Choose between standard rooms and suites (with separate lounge and kitchen) at this serviceable spot with a broad Breakaways panorama. It's a fair walk from town, but friendly and affordable. One of a few decent motel options on Catacomb Rd.

Eating

★ **John's Pizza Bar & Restaurant** ITALIAN $$
(08-8672 5561; www.johnspizzabarandrestaurant.com.au; Shop 24, 1 Hutchison St; mains $13-32; 10am-10pm) You can't go past John's, where staff serve up table-sized pizzas, hearty pastas and heat-beating gelato. Grills, salads, burgers, yiros, and fish and chips also available. Sit inside, order some takeaways, or pull up a seat with the bedraggled pot plants by the street.

Tom & Mary's Greek Taverna GREEK $$
(08-8672 5622; Shop 4/2 Hutchison St; mains $17-32; 6-9pm Mon-Sat) This busy Greek diner does everything from a superb moussaka to yiros, seafood, Greek salads and pastas with Hellenic zing. Sit back with a cold retsina as the red sun sets on another dusty day in Coober Pedy.

Information

24-hour Water Dispenser (Hutchison St; per 30L $0.20) Fill your canteens next to the visitor information centre.

Coober Pedy Hospital (08-8672 5009; www.sahealth.sa.gov.au; Lot 89 Hospital Rd; 24hr) Accident and emergency.

Coober Pedy Visitor Information Centre (1800 637 076, 08-8672 4617; www.opalcapitaloftheworld.com.au; Council Offices, Lot 773 Hutchison St; 8.30am-5pm Mon-Fri, 10am-1pm Sat & Sun) Free 30-minute internet access (prebooked), history displays and comprehensive tour and accommodation info.

Port Augusta

POP 13,900

From utilitarian Port Augusta – the 'Crossroads of Australia' – highways and railways roll west across the Nullarbor into Western Australia, north to the Flinders Ranges or Darwin, south to Adelaide or Port Lincoln, and east to Sydney. Not a bad position! The old town centre has considerable appeal, with some elegant old buildings and a revitalised waterfront: locals cast lines into the blue as Indigenous kids backflip off jetties.

Sights & Activities

Australian Arid Lands Botanic Garden GARDENS
(www.aalbg.sa.gov.au; Stuart Hwy; tour charges apply; gardens 7.30am-dusk, visitor centre 9am-5pm Mon-Fri, 10am-4pm Sat & Sun) FREE Just north of town, the excellent (and free!) botanic garden has 250 hectares of sand hills, clay flats and desert flora and fauna. Explore on your own, or take a guided tour (10am Monday to Friday). There's a cafe here too.

Port Augusta Aquatic & Outdoor Adventure Centre OUTDOORS
(08-8642 2699, 0427 722 450; www.augustaoutdoors.com.au; 4 El Alamein Rd; 9am-4pm Mon-Fri) Offers lessons and gear rental for kayaking, windsurfing, rock climbing, abseiling, snorkelling, bushwalking, sailing... Bike hire $20 per hour.

Sleeping & Eating

Shoreline Caravan Park CARAVAN PARK $
(08-8642 2965; www.shorelinecaravanpark.com.au; Gardiner Ave; unpowered/powered sites $30/33, dm $40, cabins $60-130;) It's a dusty site and a fair walk from town (and from the shoreline when the tide is out), but the cabins here are decent and there are simple four-bed dorm units for backpackers. The cheapest beds in town for those who don't fancy sleeping above a pub.

Oasis Apartments APARTMENT $$
(08-8648 9000, 1800 008 648; www.majestichotels.com.au; Marryatt St; apt $153-219;) Catering largely to conventioneers, this group of 75 luxury units (from studios to two bedrooms) with jaunty designs is right by the water. All rooms have washing machines, dryers, TVs, fridges, microwaves, fortresslike security and flashy interior design. Free wi-fi too.

JOHN WHITE PHOTOS/GETTY IMAGES ©

Jetty, Port Augusta

Crossroads Ecomotel MOTEL $$
(☎08-8642 2540; www.ecomotel.com.au; 45 Eyre Hwy; d from $120; ❄📶) 🍃 Brand new when we visited, this is one cool motel (literally). Built using rammed earth, double glazing and structural insulated panels (SIPs), the aim is to provide a thermally stable environment for guests, plus 100% more architectural style than anything else in Port Augusta. Desert hues, nice linen and free wi-fi seal the deal. A pool is on the cards.

Standpipe INDIAN $$
(☎08-8642 4033; www.standpipe.com.au; cnr Stuart Hwy & Hwy 1; mains $18-39; ⏰6-9pm) The sprawling Standpipe motel attracts government delegates and business types with its pool, adjacent golf course and 85 reasonably hip units (doubles/two-bedroom apartments from $128/233), but the main lure is the awesome (and very unexpected) Indian restaurant here. Unbelievable!

ℹ Information

Port Augusta Visitor Information Centre (☎08-8641 9193, 1800 633 060; www.portaugusta.sa.gov.au; Wadlata Outback Centre, 41 Flinders Tce; ⏰9am-5.30pm Mon-Fri, 10am-4pm Sat & Sun) This is the major information outlet for the Eyre Peninsula, Flinders Ranges and outback. It's part of the **Wadlata Outback Centre** (www.wadlata.sa.gov.au; 41 Flinders Tce; adult/child/family $19.50/11/42; ⏰9am-5.30pm Mon-Fri, 10am-4pm Sat & Sun), where the 'Tunnel of Time' traces Aboriginal and European histories using audiovisual displays, interactive exhibits and a distressingly big snake.

ADELAIDE

POP 1.29 MILLION

Sophisticated, cultured, neat-casual – this is the self-image Adelaide projects, a nod to the days of free colonisation without the penal colony taint. Adelaidians may remind you of their convict-free status, but the stuffy, affluent origins of the 'City of Churches' did more to inhibit development than promote it. Bogged down in the old-school doldrums and painfully short on charisma, this was a pious, introspective place, but these days it's a different place, with exciting food options, festivals and a funky bar scene.

Sights

★Central Market — MARKET

(www.adelaidecentralmarket.com.au; Gouger St; ⏲7am-5.30pm Tue, 9am-5.30pm Wed & Thu, 7am-9pm Fri, 7am-3pm Sat) Satisfy both obvious and obscure culinary cravings at the 250-odd stalls in Adelaide's superb Central Market. A sliver of salami from the Mettwurst Shop, a crumb of English Stilton from the Smelly Cheese Shop, a tub of blueberry yoghurt from the Yoghurt Shop – you name it, it's here. Good luck making it out without eating anything. Adelaide's Chinatown is right next door. Adelaide's Top Food & Wine Tours (p95) offers guided tours.

★Art Gallery of South Australia — GALLERY

(www.artgallery.sa.gov.au; North Tce; ⏲10am-5pm) FREE Spend a few hushed hours in the vaulted, parquetry-floored gallery that represents the big names in Australian art. Permanent exhibitions include Australian, Aboriginal and Torres Strait Islander, Asian, European and North American art (20 bronze Rodins!). Progressive visiting exhibitions occupy the basement. There are free guided tours (11am and 2pm daily) and lunchtime talks (12.30pm Tuesdays).

National Wine Centre of Australia — WINERY

(www.wineaustralia.com.au; cnr Botanic & Hackney Rds; ⏲8am-9pm Mon-Fri, 9am-9pm Sat, 9am-7am Sun, tours & tastings 10am-5pm) FREE Check out the free self-guided, interactive *Wine Discovery Journey* exhibition, paired with tastings of Australian wines (from $10), at this very sexy wine centre (actually a research facility for the University of Adelaide, rather than a visitor centre per se). You will gain an insight into the issues winemakers contend with, and can even have your own virtual vintage rated. Friday-evening 'uncorked' drinks happen at 4.30pm, and there's a cool cafe here, too.

South Australian Museum — MUSEUM

(www.samuseum.sa.gov.au; North Tce; ⏲10am-5pm) FREE Dig into Australia's natural history with the museum's special exhibits on whales and Antarctic explorer Sir Douglas Mawson. An Aboriginal Cultures Gallery displays artefacts of the Ngarrindjeri people of the Coorong and lower Murray. The giant squid and the lion with the twitchy tail are definite highlights. Free tours depart 11am weekdays and 2pm and 3pm weekends. The cafe here is a good spot for lunch.

Adelaide Zoo — ZOO

(www.zoossa.com.au/adelaide-zoo; Frome Rd; adult/child/family $32.50/18/85; ⏲9.30am-5pm) Around 1800 exotic and native mammals, birds and reptiles roar, growl and screech at Adelaide's wonderful zoo, dating from 1883. There are free walking tours half-hourly (plus a slew of longer and overnight tours), feeding sessions and a children's zoo. Wang Wang and Funi are Australia's only giant pandas – they arrived in 2009 (pandemonium!) and always draw a crowd. Other highlights include the nocturnal and reptile houses.

Adelaide Botanic Gardens — GARDENS

(www.botanicgardens.sa.gov.au; North Tce; ⏲7.15am-sunset Mon-Fri, from 9am Sat & Sun) FREE Chew through your trashy airport novel or go jogging in these lush gardens. Highlights include a restored 1877 palm house, the waterlily pavilion (housing the gigantic *Victoria amazonica*), the new First Creek wetlands, the engrossing **Museum of Economic Botany** and the fabulous steel-and-glass arc of the **Bicentennial Conservatory** (open 10am to 4pm), which recreates a tropical rainforest. Free 1½-hour guided walks depart the Schomburgk Pavilion at 10.30am daily.

West Terrace Cemetery — CEMETERY

(☎08-8139 7400; www.aca.sa.gov.au; West Tce; ⏲6.30am-6pm Nov-Apr, to 8.30pm May-Oct) FREE Driven-by and overlooked by most Adelaidians, this amazing old cemetery (established in 1837, and now with 150,000 residents) makes a serene and fascinating detour. The 2km self-guided **Heritage Highlights Interpretive Trail** meanders past 29 key sites; pick up a brochure at the West Tce entrance. Guided tours run at 10.30am Tuesday and Sunday ($10 per person); call for bookings.

Tandanya National Aboriginal Cultural Institute — GALLERY

(☎08-8224 3200; www.tandanya.com.au; 253 Grenfell St; ⏲9am-4pm Mon-Sat) FREE Tandanya offers an insight into the culture of the local Kaurna people, whose territory extends south to Cape Jervis and north to Port Wakefield. Inside are interactive visual-arts gallery spaces, plus a gift shop and a cafe.

Adelaide

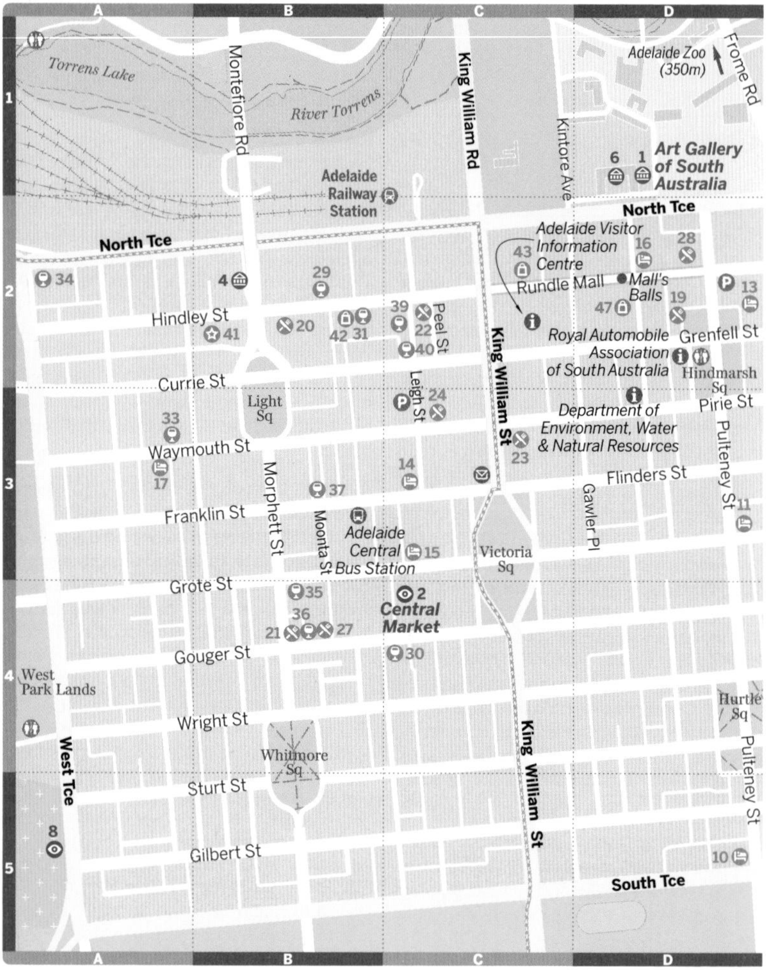

Call for info on regular didgeridoo or Torres Strait Islander cultural performances and prebooked group tours.

Adelaide Park Lands GARDENS

FREE The city centre and ritzy North Adelaide are surrounded by a broad band of parkland. Colonel William Light, Adelaide's controversial planner, came up with the concept, which has been both a blessing and a curse for the city. Pros: heaps of green space, clean air and playgrounds for the kids. Cons: bone dry in summer, loitering perverts and a sense that the city is cut off from its suburbs.

Don't miss the **playgrounds** and **Adelaide-Himeji Garden** on South Tce, and the **statue of Colonel William Light** overlooking the Adelaide Oval and city office towers from Montefiore Hill.

Jam Factory Contemporary Craft & Design Centre GALLERY

(☎08-8410 0727; www.jamfactory.com.au; 19 Morphett St; ⏲10am-5pm Mon-Sat) FREE Quality contemporary local arts and crafts, plus workshops and a hellishly hot glass-blowing studio (watch from the balcony

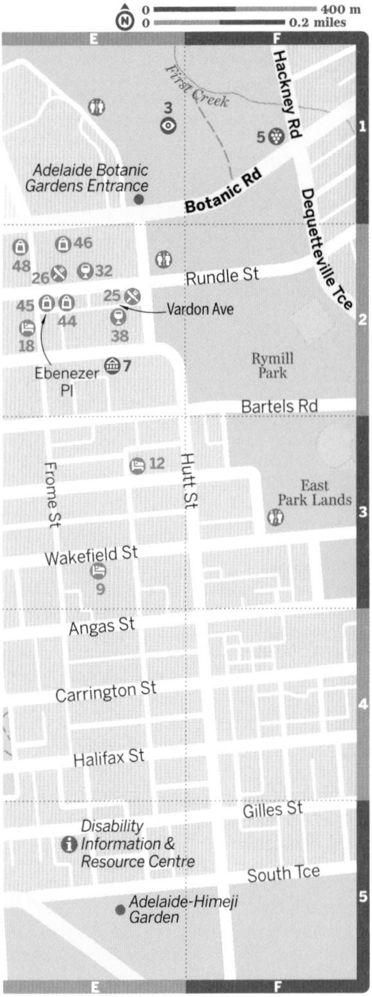

above) turning out gorgeous glass. Group tours (six or more people) by arrangement.

Activities

Adelaide is a flat town – perfect for cycling and walking (if it's not too hot!). You can take your bike on trains any time, but not on buses. **Trails SA** (www.southaustraliantrails.com) offers loads of cycling- and hiking-trail info: pick up its *40 Great South Australian Short Walks* brochure.

There are free guided walks in the Adelaide Botanic Gardens (p93). The riverside **Linear Park Trail** is a 40km walking/cycling path running from Glenelg to the foot of the Adelaide Hills, mainly along the River Torrens. Another popular hiking trail is the steep **Waterfall Gully Track** (three hours return) up to Mt Lofty Summit and back.

Escapegoat BICYCLE TOURS
(☎0422 916 289, 08-8121 8112; www.escapegoat.com.au) Ride from the 710m Mt Lofty Summit down to Adelaide ($99), or take a day trip through McLaren Vale by bike ($129). Flinders Ranges bike trips also available.

Dolphin Explorer Cruises BOATING, CRUISE
(☎08-8447 2366; www.dolphinexplorer.com.au; Commercial Rd, Port Adelaide; 2hr cruises from adult/child $10/6; ⏲daily) Cruises departing Port Adelaide's Fishermen's Wharf to ogle bottlenose dolphins in the Port River. Lots of cruise-and-dine options also available.

Tours

A great way to see Adelaide is to circle around the main sights on the free city buses. Beyond the city, day tours cover the Adelaide Hills, Fleurieu Peninsula, Barossa Valley and Clare Valley. One-day trips to the Flinders Ranges and Kangaroo Island tend to be rushed and not great value for money.

Adelaide's Top Food & Wine Tours TOUR
(☎08-8386 0888; www.topfoodandwinetours.com.au) Uncovers SA's gastronomic soul with dawn ($70 including breakfast) and morning ($55) tours of the buzzing Central Market where stallholders introduce their produce. Adelaide Hills, McLaren Vale, Barossa and Clare Valley wine tours are also available.

Bookabee Tours CULTURAL TOUR
(☎08-8235 9954; www.bookabee.com.au) Indigenous-run half-/full-day city tours ($180/255) focusing on bush foods in the Adelaide Botanic Gardens, Tandanya National Aboriginal Cultural Institute and the South Australian Museum. A great insight into Kaurna culture. Longer Flinders Ranges tours also available.

Adelaide Sightseeing GUIDED TOUR
(☎1300 769 762; www.adelaidesightseeing.com.au) Runs a city highlights tour ($64) including North Tce, Glenelg, Haigh's Chocolates and the Adelaide Oval (among other sights). Central Market, Barossa Valley, McLaren Vale, Adelaide Hills and Kangaroo Island tours also available.

Adelaide

Festivals & Events

Tour Down Under SPORTS
(www.tourdownunder.com.au) The world's best cyclists sweating in their lycra: six races through SA towns, with the grand finale in Adelaide in January.

Adelaide Fringe ARTS
(www.adelaidefringe.com.au) This annual independent arts festival in February and March is second only to the Edinburgh Fringe. Funky, unpredictable and downright hilarious.

Adelaide Festival ARTS
(www.adelaidefestival.com.au) Top-flight international and Australian dance, drama, opera, literature and theatre performances in March. Don't miss the Northern Lights along North Tce – old sandstone buildings ablaze with lights – and Lola's Pergola late-night club.

WOMADelaide MUSIC
(www.womadelaide.com.au) One of the world's best live-music events, with more than 300 musicians and performers from around the globe. In March.

Tasting Australia FOOD, WINE
(www.tastingaustralia.com.au) SA foodie experiences around the city, categorised as either 'Eat', Drink', 'Share' or 'Think'. Classes, demonstrations and lots to put in your mouth. Held in late April.

Sleeping

Accommodation is plentiful in the city centre. See www.bandbfsa.com.au for B&B listings.

My Place HOSTEL $
(☎1800 221 529, 08-8221 5299; www.adelaidehostel.com.au; 257 Waymouth St; dm/tw/d incl breakfast from $26/72/72; P ❄ 📶) The antithesis of the big formal operations, My Place has a welcoming, personal vibe and is just a stumble from the Grace Emily, arguably Adelaide's best pub. There's a cosy TV room, a barbecue terrace above the street, free bikes and

wi-fi, hiking trips and regular pizza and pub nights – great for solo travellers.

Backpack Oz HOSTEL $
(1800 633 307, 08-8223 3551; www.backpackoz.com.au; cnr Wakefield & Pulteney Sts; dm/s/d/tw/tr $26/65/70/75/105;) It doesn't look like much externally, but this converted pub (the old Orient Hotel) strikes the right balance between party and placid. There are spacious dorms and an additional no-frills guesthouse over the road (good for couples). Get a coldie and shoot some pool in the bar. Lots of free stuff, too: breakfast, wi-fi, bikes, linen and Wednesday night BBQ.

Hotel Metropolitan PUB $
(08-8231 5471; www.hotelmetro.com.au; 46 Grote St; s/tw/d/f from $55/90/90/180;) The 1883 Metropolitan pub has 26 rooms upstairs, with stripy linen, high ceilings, little flat-screen TVs and various bedding configurations. 'It used to be quite an experience staying here...' says the barman, raising his eyebrows. We're not sure what he meant, but these days you can expect a decent budget sleep in a beaut location. Shared bathrooms.

★ **Adabco Boutique Hotel** BOUTIQUE HOTEL $$
(08-8100 7500; www.adabcohotel.com.au; 223 Wakefield St; d from $139;) This excellent, stone-clad boutique hotel – built in 1894 in high Venetian Gothic style – has at various times been an Aboriginal education facility, a rollerskating rink and an abseiling venue! These days you can expect three levels of lovely rooms with interesting art and quality linen, plus complimentary breakfast, free wi-fi and smiling staff. A top choice.

Hotel Richmond HOTEL $$
(08-8215 4444; www.hotelrichmond.com.au; 128 Rundle Mall; d from $140;) This opulent hotel in a grand 1920s building in the middle of Rundle Mall has mod-minimalist rooms with king-sized beds, marble bathrooms, and American oak and Italian furnishings. Oh, and that hotel rarity – opening windows. Rates include movies and newspapers. Parking from $20 per day.

Clarion Hotel Soho HOTEL $$
(08-8412 5600; www.clarionhotelsoho.com.au; 264 Flinders St; d from $145;) Attempting to conjure up the vibe of London's Soho district, these plush suites in Adelaide's East End (some with spas, most with balconies) are complemented by sumptuous linen, 24-hour room service, Italian marble bathrooms, jet pool and a fab restaurant. Rates take a tumble midweek. Parking from $20; free wi-fi.

Franklin Central Apartments APARTMENTS $$
(1300 662 288, 08-8221 7050; www.franklinapartments.com.au; 36 Franklin St; 1-/2-/3-bedroom apt from $148/199/298;) This old redbrick office building has heaps of charm, and now houses five levels of good-value downtown apartments with smart interiors. The marketing angle sways towards corporate,

LOCAL KNOWLEDGE

ADELAIDE ARTS & FESTIVALS

Emma Fey, Adelaide arts doyen and former Development Manager at the Art Gallery of South Australia, filled us in on some highlights of Adelaide's festival calendar and arts scene.

Festival Season

The Adelaide Festival, the Fringe Festival, Adelaide Writers' Week and the Clipsal 500 (V8 race) all happen around February/March. Energy breeds energy: everyone is out and about and the weather's good. I can't think of anywhere else where you can see alternative Fringe-dwellers next to racing enthusiasts. The people-watching is great!

Art in the City

The Art Gallery of South Australia is in the middle of the North Tce precinct (next to the museum and the university, between the city and the river). The gallery has refurbished and rehung its Elder and Melrose wings, and is engaging a wider audience – especially young people and children with a new dedicated art-making space called the Studio. There are also contemporary art spaces popping up in little lanes around the precinct.

Best Free Events

All sorts of amazing free events appear around the city, especially during the Adelaide Festival. Guerrilla street art teamed with pop-up dining experiences, the sensational Adelaide Festival late-night club Lola's Pergola, and the Art Gallery of SA's free daily programs.

but the location and rates spell 'h-o-l-i-d-a-y'. Parking $15 per day.

Adelaide City Park Motel MOTEL $$
(☎08-8223 1444; www.citypark.com.au; 471 Pulteney St; d with/without bathroom from $110/88, f from $210; P ❄ ☎) One of the better motels around town (there are surprisingly few that pass muster), with immaculate bathrooms, leather lounges and winsome French prints. An easy walk to the Hutt St restaurants, and well-placed for the freeway to the Adelaide Hills and Melbourne. Free parking, DVDs and wi-fi, too.

Crowne Plaza Adelaide HOTEL $$
(☎08-8206 8888; www.crowneplaza.com/adelaide; 16 Hindmarsh Sq; d from $180; P ❄ @ ☎ ≋) The Crowne Plaza spreads itself through two 14-storey towers just back from Rundle St, with little balconies overlooking the neat lawn-scapes of Hindmarsh Sq. Don't expect anything too soulful: it's a slick, corporate, international set-up… But the location is primo. Parking $36 per day.

Roof Garden Hotel HOTEL $$$
(☎1800 008 499, 08-8100 4400; www.majestichotels.com.au; 55 Frome St; d from $200; P ❄ @ ☎) Everything looks new in this central, Japanese-themed place. Book a room facing Frome St for a balcony and the best views, or take a bottle of wine up to the namesake rooftop garden to watch the sunset. Free wi-fi and good walk-in and last-minute rates. Parking from $20 per day.

Eating

Foodies flock to West End hotspots such as Gouger St (pronounced 'goo-jer'), Chinatown and the food-filled Central Market. There are some great pubs here too. Arty/alternative Hindley St – Adelaide's dirty little secret – has a smattering of good eateries. In the East End, Rundle St and Hutt St offer alfresco cafes and people-watching. North Adelaide's Melbourne and O'Connell Sts have a healthy spread of bistros, cafes and pubs.

Central Market MARKET $
(www.adelaidecentralmarket.com.au; Gouger St; ⏲7am-5.30pm Tue, 9am-5.30pm Wed & Thu, 7am-9pm Fri, 7am-3pm Sat) This place is an exercise in sensory bombardment: a barrage of smells, colours and yodelling stallholders selling fresh vegetables, breads, cheeses, seafood and gourmet produce. Cafes, hectic food courts, a supermarket and Adelaide's Chinatown are here, too.

Zen Kitchen VIETNAMESE $
(☎08-8232 3542; www.facebook.com/zenkitchenadelaide; Unit 7, Tenancy 2, Renaissance Arc; mains $5-11; ⏲10.30am-4.30pm Mon-Thu, 10.30am-8pm Fri, 11am-3pm Sat) Superb, freshly constructed cold rolls, *pho* soups and super-crunchy barbecue-pork bread rolls, eat-in or takeaway. Wash it all down with a cold coconut milk or a teeth-grindingly strong Vietnamese coffee with sugary condensed milk. Authentic, affordable and delicious.

Lucia's Pizza & Spaghetti Bar ITALIAN $
(☎08-8231 2260; www.lucias.com.au; 2 Western Mall, Central Market; meals $8-14; ⏲7am-4pm Mon-Thu & Sat, to 9pm Fri) This little slice of Italy has been around since Lucia was a lot younger. All her pasta, sauces and pizzas are authentically homemade. If you like what you're eating, you can buy fresh pasta next door at Lucia's Fine Foods.

Vego And Loven' It VEGETARIAN $
(www.vegoandlovenit.webs.com; Level 1, 240 Rundle St; meals $7-14; ⏲10am-4pm Mon-Fri; ✎) Get your weekly vitamins disguised in a scrumptious veggie burger, wrap or focaccia at this arty upstairs kitchen. Dreadlocked urban renegades order 'extra alfalfa but no hummus'. Look for the mosaic sign and take the skinny stairs.

Jerusalem Sheshkabab House MIDDLE EASTERN $
(☎08-8212 6185; 131b Hindley St; mains $10-15; ⏲noon-2pm & 5.30-10pm Tue-Sun; ✎) A skinny Hindley St room that's been here forever, serving magnificent Middle Eastern and Lebanese delights: falafels, hummus, tabouleh, tahini and (of course) sheshkababs. The plastic furniture and draped tent material are appropriately tacky.

★ **Peel Street** MODERN AUSTRALIAN, ASIAN $$
(☎08-8231 8887; www.peelst.com.au; 9 Peel St; mains $20-30, tasting menu $68; ⏲7.30am-3pm Mon-Fri, 6.30pm-late Thu-Sat) A long-neglected service lane in Adelaide's West End, Peel St has spawned a slew of new bar-eateries recently, the first (and still best) of which is Peel Street itself, a supercool cafe-bistro–wine bar that just keeps packing 'em in. Glam city girls sit at window seats nibbling parmesan-crumbed parsnips and turkey meatballs with preserved lemon. Killer wine list.

Pizza e Mozzarella Bar ITALIAN $$
(☎08-8164 1003; www.pizzaemozzarellabar.com.au; 33 Pirie St; pizzas $19-23, mains $20-36; ⏲11.30am-3pm Mon-Thu, 1.30-9.30pm Fri, 5.30-9.30pm Sat) Everything at this split-level,

Moving grapes in the Barossa Valley, South Australia's key wine-growing region

rustic Italian eatery – adorned with bread baskets and terracotta; beautified by Italian staff and leadlight – is cooked in the wood oven you see when you walk in the door. Pizzas are thin-based (Roma style); mozzarella plates come with wood-oven bread and meats (octopus, tuna, salumi). Super Italian/SA wine and beer list. Just super!

Jasmin Indian Restaurant INDIAN $$
(☑08-8223 7837; www.jasmin.com.au; basement, 31 Hindmarsh Sq; mains $17-29; ⊘noon-2.30pm Thu & Fri, 5.30-9pm Tue-Sat) Magical North Indian curries and consummately professional staff (they might remember your name from when you ate here in 2011). There's nothing too surprising about the menu, but it's done to absolute perfection. Bookings essential.

Mesa Lunga MEDITERRANEAN $$
(☑08-8410 7617; www.mesalunga.com; cnr Gouger & Morphett Sts; tapas $4-19, mains $18-31; ⊘noon-3pm Fri, noon-late Sun, 6pm-late Tue-Sat) In a fishbowl corner room with a dark-wood wine wall, sassy Mesa Lunga serves tapas and quality pizzas. Order some *gamba* (black-salted prawn and chorizo in pastry) and Manzanillo olives stuffed with anchovies, washed down with some sparkling sangria. Magic.

Ying Chow CHINESE $$
(☑08-8211 7998; 114 Gouger St; mains $11-24; ⊘noon-2.45pm Fri, 5pm-midnight daily) This fluoro-lit, bossy-staffed eatery is a culinary gem; serving cuisine styled from the Guangzhou region, such as 'BBC' (bean curd, broad beans and Chinese chutney) and steamed duck with salty sauce. It gets packed – with queues out the door (no bookings) – but it's worth the wait.

★**Press** MODERN AUSTRALIAN $$$
(☑08-8211 8048; www.pressfoodandwine.com.au; 40 Waymouth St; mains $16-48; ⊘noon-late Mon-Sat) The best of an emerging strip of restaurants on office-heavy Waymouth St. Super-stylish (brick, glass, lemon-coloured chairs) and not afraid of offal (pan-fried lamb's brains, grilled calf's tongue) or things raw (beef carpaccio, gravlax salmon) and confit (duck leg, onion, olives). Tasting menu $68 per person. Book for upstairs seating only; otherwise they'll fit you downstairs near the bar.

Sosta ARGENTINE $$$
(☑08-8232 6799; www.sostaargentiniankitchen.com.au; 291 Rundle St; tapas $16-26, mains $33-45; ⊘noon-2.30pm Mon-Fri, 6pm-late daily) Beef, lamb, pork, chicken, fish...vegetarians run

for the hills! Sosta's aged 1kg T-bone steaks are legendary. With crisp white tablecloths and blood-brown floorboards, it's an elegant place to launch your nocturnal East End foray.

Drinking & Nightlife

Rundle St has a few iconic pubs, while in the West End, Hindley St's red-light sleaze collides with the hip bars on Leigh and Peel Sts. Cover charges at clubs can be anything from free to $15, depending on the night. Most clubs close Monday to Thursday.

★Exeter Hotel PUB
(☎08-8223 2623; www.facebook.com; 246 Rundle St; ⏲8am-late) Adelaide's best pub, this legendary boozer attracts an eclectic mix of postwork, punk and uni drinkers, shaking the day off their backs. Pull up a stool at the bar, or a table in the grungy beer garden, and settle in for the evening. Original music nightly (indie, electronica, acoustic); no pokies. Book for curry nights in the upstairs restaurant (usually Wednesdays).

★Grace Emily Hotel PUB
(www.graceemilyhotel.com.au; 232 Waymouth St; ⏲4pm-late) Duking it out with the Exeter Hotel for the title of 'Adelaide's Best Pub' (it pains us to separate the two) the Gracie has live music most nights (alt-rock, country, acoustic, open-mic nights), kooky '50s-meets-voodoo decor, open fires and great beers. Regular cult cinema; no pokies. Are the Bastard Sons of Ruination playing tonight?

Downtown HDCB BAR
(☎08-8212 7334; www.facebook.com/Downtown-HDCB; 99 Hindley St; ⏲noon-midnight Wed-Fri, 6pm-2am Sat) HDCB equals Hot Dogs, Cold Beer. You'll find plenty of each inside this slender Hindley St bar, plus walls spangled with vintage music posters and tattooed DJs playing rock and hip-hop. It's something different for Hindley St – a beacon of grit and substance amid the strip clubs, fluoro-lit convenience stores, sex shops and mainstream beer barns.

> **PINT OF COOPERS PLEASE!**
>
> Things can get confusing at the bar in Adelaide. Aside from the 200mL (7oz) 'butchers' – the choice of old men in dim, sticky-carpet pubs – there are three main beer sizes: 285mL (10oz) 'schooners' (pots or middies elsewhere in Australia), 425mL (15oz) 'pints' (schooners elsewhere) and 568mL (20oz) 'imperial pints' (traditional English pints). Now go forth and order with confidence!

Cork Wine Cafe WINE BAR
(www.corkwinecafe.com.au; 61a Gouger St; ⏲4pm-midnight Mon-Thu, 3pm-1am Fri & Sat) A down-sized, Frenchie hole-in-the-wall wine bar, unexpected among the fluoro-lit Chinese restaurants along this stretch of Gouger St. Well-worn floorboards, Bentwood chairs, absinthe posters...perfect for a quick vino before dinner.

Udaberri BAR
(www.udaberri.com.au; 11-13 Leigh St; ⏲4pm-late Tue-Thu, 3pm-late Fri, 6pm-late Sat) Taking a leaf out of the Melbourne book on laneside boozing, nouveau-industrial Udaberri is a compact bar on Leigh St, serving Spanish wines by the glass, good beers on tap and *pintxos* (Basque bar snacks) like oysters, cheeses, *jamon* and tortillas. The crowd is cashed-up and city-centric.

Apothecary 1878 WINE BAR
(www.theapothecary1878.com.au; 118 Hindley St; ⏲5pm-late) Classy coffee and wine at this gorgeous chemist-turned-bar, dating from (you guessed it) 1878. Dark-timber medicine cabinets and Parisian marble-topped tables: perfect first-date territory.

Tasting Room WINE BAR
(www.eastendcellars.com.au; 25 Vardon Ave; ⏲9am-7pm Mon & Tue, 9am-9pm Wed & Thu, 9am-10pm Fri, 10am-10pm Sat, noon-7pm Sun) A commercial offshoot of East End Cellars, Adelaide's best bottle shop, this classy new wine room gives you the chance to try before you buy. The range is vast: prop yourself on a window seat, watch beautiful East Enders sashay past, and work your way through it.

Publishers Hotel BAR
(www.publishershotel.com.au; cnr Cannon & Franklin Sts; ⏲11am-late Tue-Sat, 3pm-late Sun) 'Established 1914' says the signage. By our reckoning it was closer to 2014... Either way, the Publishers of today is an upmarket bar with white-jacketed bartenders, interesting wines and craft beers (love the Lobethal Bierhaus pilsner from the Adelaide Hills). Weekend DJs spin everything from old soul to Dire Straits (the vibe is very over-30s).

River Torrens, Elder Park and Adelaide CBD

Zhivago CLUB
(www.zhivago.com.au; 54 Currie St; ⏲9pm-late Fri-Sun) The pick of the West End clubs (there are quite a few of 'em around Light Sq – some are a bit moron-prone), Zhivago's DJs pump out everything from reggae and dub to quality house. Popular with the 18 to 25 dawn patrol.

Lotus Lounge CLUB
(www.lotuslounge.net.au; 268 Morphett St; ⏲6pm-late Wed-Sat) We like the signage here – a very minimal fluoro martini glass with a flashing olive. Inside it's a glam lounge with cocktails, quality beers and Adelaide dolls cuttin' the rug. Expect queues around the corner on Saturday nights.

HQ Complex CLUB
(www.hqcomplex.com.au; 1 North Tce; ⏲8pm-late Wed, Fri & Sat) Adelaide's biggest club fills five big rooms with shimmering sound and light. Night-time is the right time on Saturdays – the biggest (and trashiest) club night in town. Retro Wednesdays; live acts Fridays.

Mars Bar CLUB
(www.themarsbar.com.au; 120 Gouger St; ⏲9pm-late Fri & Sat) The lynchpin of Adelaide's nocturnal gay and lesbian scene, always-busy Mars Bar features glitzy decor, flashy clientele and OTT drag shows.

☆ Entertainment

Arty Adelaide has a rich cultural life that stacks up favourably with much larger cities.

For listings and reviews see **Adelaide Now** (www.adelaidenow.com.au) and **Adelaide Review** (www.adelaidereview.com.au).

There are a few agencies for big-ticket event bookings:

BASS (☎13 12 46; www.bass.net.au)

Moshtix (☎1300 438 849; www.moshtix.com.au)

Venue Tix (☎08-8225 8888; www.venuetix.com.au)

Live Music

Adelaide knows how to kick out the jams! Top pub venues around town include the Grace Emily (p100) and Exeter Hotel (p100).

Adelaide Festival (p96)

The free street-press papers *Rip It Up* (www.ripitup.com.au) and *dB* (www.dbmagazine.com.au) have band and DJ listings and reviews. For gig listings see **Music SA** (www.musicsa.com.au) and **Jazz Adelaide** (www.jazz.adelaide.onau.net).

★ **Governor Hindmarsh Hotel** LIVE MUSIC
(www.thegov.com.au; 59 Port Rd, Hindmarsh; ⏲ 11am-late) Ground Zero for live music in Adelaide, the Gov hosts some legendary local and international acts. The odd Irish band fiddles around in the bar, while the main venue features rock, folk, jazz, blues, salsa, reggae and dance. A huge place with an inexplicably personal vibe. Good food, too.

Jive LIVE MUSIC
(www.jivevenue.com; 181 Hindley St; ⏲ hours vary) In a converted theatre, Jive caters to an offbeat crowd of student types who like their tunes funky, left-field and removed from the mainstream. A sunken dance floor = great views from the bar!

Shopping

Shops and department stores line Rundle Mall. The beautiful old arcades between the mall and Grenfell St retain their original splendour and house eclectic little shops. Rundle St and the adjunct Ebenezer Pl are home to boutique and retro clothing shops.

★ **Streetlight** BOOKS, MUSIC
(www.facebook.com/streetlightadelaide; 2/15 Vaughan Pl; ⏲ 10am-6pm Mon-Thu & Sat, 10am-9pm Fri, 11am-5pm Sun) Lefty, arty and subversive in the best possible way, Streetlight is the place to find that elusive Miles Davis disc or Charles Bukowski poetry compilation.

Midwest Trader CLOTHING, ACCESSORIES
(www.facebook.com; Shop 1 & 2 Ebenezer Pl; ⏲ 10am-6pm Mon-Thu & Sat, 10am-9pm Fri, noon-5pm Sun) Stocks a snarling range of punk, skate, vintage, biker and rockabilly gear, plus secondhand cowboy boots. Rock on!

Imprints Booksellers BOOKS
(www.imprints.com.au; 107 Hindley St; ⏲ 9am-6pm Mon-Wed, 9am-9pm Thu & Fri, 9am-5pm Sat, 11am-5pm Sun) The best bookshop in Adelaide in the worst location (in the thick of the Hindley St strip-club fray)? Jazz, floorboards, Persian rugs and occasional live readings and book launches.

Urban Cow Studio DESIGN
(www.urbancow.com.au; 11 Frome St; ⌚10am-6pm Mon-Thu, 10am-9pm Fri, 10am-5pm Sat, noon-5pm Sun) The catch cry here is 'Handmade in Adelaide' – a brilliant assortment of paintings, jewellery, glassware, ceramics and textiles, plus a gallery upstairs. Their 'Heaps Good' T-shirts are appropriately pro-SA on a hot summer's day.

Miss Gladys Sym Choon FASHION
(www.missgladyssymchoon.com.au; 235a Rundle St; ⌚9.30am-6.15pm Mon-Thu, 9.30am-9.30pm Fri, 10am-6pm Sat, 10.45am-5.30pm Sun) Named after a famed Rundle St trader from the 1920s, this hip shop is the place for fab frocks, rockin' boots, street-beating sneakers, jewellery, watches and hats.

Jurlique COSMETICS
(www.jurlique.com.au; Shop 2Ga, 50 Rundle Mall Plaza; ⌚9am-6pm Mon-Thu, 9am-9pm Fri, 9am-5pm Sat, 11am-5pm Sun) An international success story, SA's own Jurlique sells fragrant skincare products (some Rosewater Balancing Mist, anyone?) that are pricey but worth every cent.

Tarts DESIGN
(www.tartscollective.com.au; 10g Gays Arcade, Adelaide Arcade, Rundle Mall; ⌚10am-5pm Mon-Sat) Textiles, jewellery, bags, cards and canvasses from a 35-member local arts co-op. Meet the artists in-store.

Information

EMERGENCY

Ambulance, Fire, Police (☎000) Adelaide's main police station is at 60 Wakefield St.

RAA Emergency Roadside Assistance (☎13 11 11; www.raa.com.au) Car break-down assistance.

INTERNET ACCESS

Arena Internet Café (Level 1, 264 Rundle St; ⌚11am-midnight Mon-Thu, 10am-late Fri-Sun)

Wireless Cafe (53 Hindley St; ⌚7am-7.30pm Mon-Fri, 8am-6pm Sat) Hindley St hotspot.

MEDIA

Adelaide's daily tabloid is the parochial *Advertiser*, though the *Age*, *Australian* and *Financial Review* are also widely available.

Adelaide Review (www.adelaidereview.com.au) Highbrow articles, culture and arts. Free monthly.

Blaze (www.gaynewsnetwork.com.au) Gay-and-lesbian street press; free fortnightly.

dB (www.dbmagazine.com.au) Local street press; loaded with music info.

Rip it Up (www.ripitup.com.au) Rival street press to dB; buckets of music info plus eating and drinking reviews.

MEDICAL SERVICES

Emergency Dental Service (☎08-8222 8222; www.sadental.sa.gov.au) Sore tooth?

Midnight Pharmacy (☎08-8231 6333; 13 West Tce; ⌚7am-midnight Mon-Sat, 9am-midnight Sun) Late-night subscriptions.

Royal Adelaide Hospital (☎08-8222 4000; www.rah.sa.gov.au; 275 North Tce; ⌚24hr) Emergency department (not for blisters!) and STD clinic.

Women's & Children's Hospital (☎08-8161 7000; www.cywhs.sa.gov.au; 72 King William Rd, North Adelaide; ⌚24hr) Emergency and sexual-assault services.

MONEY

American Express (www.americanexpress.com; 147 Rundle Mall, Citi Centre Arcade; ⌚9am-5pm Mon-Fri, to noon Sat) Foreign currency exchange.

Travelex (www.travelex.com.au; HSBC, 55 Grenfell St; ⌚9.30am-4pm Mon-Thu, to 5pm Fri) Foreign currency exchange in the HSBC building.

POST

Adelaide General Post Office (GPO; www.auspost.com.au; 141 King William St; ⌚9am-5.30pm Mon-Fri) Adelaide's main (and rather stately) post office.

TOURIST INFORMATION

Adelaide Visitor Information Centre (☎1300 588 140; www.adelaidecitycouncil.com; 9 James Pl, off Rundle Mall; ⌚9am-5pm Mon-Fri, 10am-4pm Sat & Sun, 11am-3pm public holidays) Adelaide-specific information, plus abundant info on SA including fab regional booklets.

Department of Environment, Water & Natural Resources (DEWNR; ☎08-8204 1910; www.environment.sa.gov.au; Level 1, 100 Pirie St; ⌚9am-5pm Mon-Fri) National parks information and bookings.

Disability Information & Resource Centre (DIRC; ☎1300 305 558, 08-8236 0555; www.dircsa.org.au; 195 Gilles St; ⌚10am-4pm Mon-Fri) Info on accommodation, venues and travel for people with disabilities.

Outback New South Wales

New South Wales (NSW) is rarely credited for its far-west outback corner, but it should be. Out here, grey saltbush and red sand make it easy to imagine yourself superimposed onto the world's biggest Aboriginal dot painting, a canvas reaching as far as the eye can see.

Bathurst

POP 31,294

Bathurst is Australia's oldest inland settlement, boasting a cool climate and a beautiful manicured central square where formidable Victorian buildings transport you to the past. And then, in a dramatic change of pace, it's also the bastion of Australian motor sport.

Sights

Ask at the visitor centre for information about wineries, hiking trails and scenic drives in the region.

★Australian Fossil & Mineral Museum MUSEUM
(www.somervillecollection.com.au; 224 Howick St; adult/child $12/6; ⏲10am-4pm Mon-Sat, to 2pm Sun) Don't let the dry name fool you – this place is a treasure chest full of wonder. It's home to the internationally renowned Somerville Collection: rare fossils, plus gemstones and minerals in every colour of the rainbow. The museum also houses Australia's only complete *Tyrannosaurus rex* skeleton.

Courthouse HISTORIC BUILDING, MUSEUM
(www.bathursthistory.org.au; Russell St; museum adult/child $4/2.50; ⏲museum 10am-4pm Tue-Sat, 11am-2pm Sun) This 1880 building is the most impressive of Bathurst's historical structures. Its east wing houses the small **Historical Museum**.

Mt Panorama LANDMARK
(www.mount-panorama.com.au) FREE Rev-heads will enjoy the 6.2km **Mt Panorama Motor Racing Circuit**, venue for the epic Bathurst 1000 V8 race each October (which sees crowds of up to 200,000). It's a public road, so you can drive around the circuit – but only up to an unthrilling 60km/h.

National Motor Racing Museum MUSEUM
(www.nmrm.com.au; Murrays Corner, Mt Panorama; adult/child $12.50/5.50; ⏲9am-4.30pm) Sits at the base of Mt Panorama and celebrates all things motor sports.

Festivals & Events

Bathurst 1000 MOTOR RACING
(www.v8supercars.com.au; ⏲Oct) Petrol-heads throng to Bathurst for this 1000km touring-car race, considered the pinnacle of Australian motor sport. It's completed over 161 laps of Mt Panorama.

Sleeping

Jack Duggans Irish Pub PUB $
(☎02-6331 2712; www.jackduggans.com.au; 135 George St; dm/s/d with shared bathroom $30/50/65) This lively spot in the heart of town has a good restaurant and bar downstairs (run by a real Irishman, with live music on weekends and good *craic*). Upstairs are small, high-quality budget rooms.

Accommodation Warehouse APARTMENTS $$
(☎02-6332 2801; www.accomwarehouse.com.au; 121a Keppel St; s/d $100/130; ❄📶) A three-level woollen mill dating from the 1870s has been cleverly converted into these five self-contained apartments. They're not slick; they're sweet and cosy and have considerably more character than a modern motel room. It's down a lane, arrowed off Keppel St.

Rydges Mount Panorama HOTEL $$
(☎02-6338 1888; www.rydges.com/bathurst; 1 Conrod Straight; r from $150; 📶🏊) Large (129 studios and apartments) and smartly furnished, with loads of facilities. Every room has a view over the racetrack, but you'll need to book well ahead for the Bathurst 1000.

Eating & Drinking

Church Bar PIZZA $$
(1 Ribbon Gang Lane; pizzas $17-25; ⏰noon-midnight) This restored 1850s church now attracts punters praying to a different deity: the god of wood-fired pizza. The soaring ceilings and verdant courtyard off William St make it one of the town's best eating and socialising venues.

Hub CAFE $$
(52 Keppel St; mains $13-25; ⏰7am-5pm Mon-Sat, to 3pm Sun) On a strip with a few cool cafe options, the courtyard canopy of red umbrellas and green leaves makes this popular spot the perfect place for an alfresco meal.

Webb & Co BAR
(www.webbandco.com.au; off George St; ⏰3pm-late Mon-Sat, noon-10pm Sun) Tucked down a central arcade (next to Crema coffee bar), this classy 'beverage emporium' proffers great craft beer, cocktails and local wine, plus a most excellent menu of share plates, mains ($26) and grazing feasts.

Information

Visitor Centre (☎02-6332 1444; www.visitbathurst.com.au; Kendall Ave; ⏰9am-5pm)

Mudgee

POP 9830

Mudgee is a pretty little pocket of New South Wales, surrounded by vineyards and rolling hills. Wineries and excellent food make Mudgee a lovely spot to relax and refuel.

Sights

Mudgee's 35 cellar doors (all family-owned operations) are primarily clustered north-east of town. Get details from the visitor centre: some vineyards have outstanding restaurants, some have accommodation, some open weekends only.

★**Lowe Wines** WINERY
(☎03-6372 0800; www.lowewine.com.au; Tinja Lane; ⏰10am-5pm) You can follow a walking/cycling trail through the orchards and vines of this idyllic organic farm, past donkeys and chickens to picnic grounds. The cellar door has tastings and a superb grazing platter ($30) of local flavours, and Zin House (p106) is on the grounds. Check the website for events, too.

Logan Wines WINERY
(www.loganwines.com.au; 33 Castlereagh Hwy; ⏰10am-5pm) An impressive and modern cellar-door experience 15km east of Mudgee.

Pieter van Gent Winery & Vineyard WINERY
(www.pvgwinery.com.au; 141 Black Springs Rd; ⏰9am-5pm Mon-Sat, 10.30am-4pm Sun) Heavenly white port and muscat, and tastings in a photogenic oak-barrel room.

Robert Stein Winery & Vineyard WINERY
(www.robertstein.com.au; Pipeclay Lane; ⏰10am-4.30pm) A small, rustic cellar door plus a vintage motorcycle museum (free). There's also an excellent paddock-to-plate restaurant, Pipeclay Pumphouse.

di Lusso Estate WINERY
(www.dilusso.com.au; 162 Eurunderee Lane; ⏰10am-5pm Mon-Sat, to 4pm Sun) Play bocce, taste-test home-grown olives and figs, eat pizza and sample Italian wine varietals (nebbiolo, sangiovese etc) at this sweet slice of Italy.

Sleeping

Mudgee Riverside Tourist Park CAMPGROUND, CABINS $
(☎02-6372 2531; www.mudgeeriverside.com.au; 22 Short St; sites $24-31, cabins from $90; ❄) Super-central, leafy and well run.

★**Perry Street Hotel** BOUTIQUE HOTEL $$
(☎02-6372 7650; www.perrystreethotel.com.au; cnr Perry & Gladstone Sts; ste from $165; ❄📶) Stunning apartment suites make a sophisticated choice in town. The attention to detail is outstanding, right down to the kimono bathrobes, Nespresso machine and free gourmet snacks.

MUDGEE WINES AT A GLANCE

- Best sources of information: **visitor centre** (the *Mudgee Region* booklet has a great map); the website www.mudgeewine.com.au
- Best winery tours: **Mudgee Wine & Country Tours** (☎ 02-6372 2367; www.mudgeewinetours.com.au; half-/full-day wine tours $50/80) and **Mudgee Tourist Bus** (☎ 02-6372 4475; www.mudgeetouristbus.com.au; half-/full-day wine tours $45/70)
- Best wine bar: **Roth's** (see below)
- Best time to visit: September for the Mudgee Wine & Food Festival

Cobb & Co Boutique Hotel BOUTIQUE HOTEL $$
(☎ 02-6372 7245; www.cobbandcocourt.com.au; 97 Market St; r from $160;) In the centre of town, this place has mod cons elegantly suited to its heritage style. Two-night minimum stay on weekends.

Eating & Drinking

Alby & Esthers CAFE $$
(www.albyandesthers.com.au; 61 Market St; mains $10-18; 8am-5pm Mon-Thu, to late Fri & Sat) Down an alleyway is this supremely pretty courtyard cafe, serving up fine local produce and good coffee. It morphs into a wine bar on Friday and Saturday nights.

★ **Zin House** MODERN AUSTRALIAN $$$
(☎ 02-6372 1660; www.zinhouse.com.au; 329 Tinja Lane; lunch $75; from 5.30pm Fri, from noon Sat & Sun) The glorious Lowe (p105) vineyard is home to this weekend highlight: long, leisurely six-course lunches of simply prepared local produce. Diners share farmhouse tables in a beautifully designed home. You can also enjoy Friday night tapas here ($45). Gather your friends; book ahead.

★ **Roth's** WINE BAR
(www.rothswinebar.com.au; 30 Market St; 5pm-midnight Wed-Sat) The oldest wine bar (1923) in NSW sits behind a small heritage facade, and serves up great local wines (by the glass from $6), fine bar food and excellent live music. Bliss.

Information

Visitor Centre (☎ 02-6372 1020; www.visitmudgeeregion.com.au; 84 Market St; 9am-5pm)

Dubbo

POP 32,300

The important rural centre of Dubbo is on one of the main inland north–south driving routes and is a gateway of sorts to the outback.

Sights

★ **Taronga Western Plains Zoo** ZOO
(☎ 02-6881 1400; www.taronga.org.au; Obley Rd; 2-day passes adult/child $47/24; 9am-4pm) This is Dubbo's star attraction, not to mention one of the best zoos in regional Australia. You can walk the 6km circuit, hire a bike ($15) or drive your car, getting out at enclosures along the way. Guided walks (adult/child $15/7.50) start at 6.45am on weekends (additional days in school holidays). There are free barbecues and picnic grounds at the zoo, as well as cafes and kiosks. Book ahead for special animal encounters, or for the glorious accommodation packages – spend a night at a bush camp, in family-sized cabins or safari-style lodges, overlooking savannah.

Western Plains Cultural Centre MUSEUM
(www.wpccdubbo.org.au; 76 Wingewarra St; 10am-4pm Wed-Sun) FREE Housing Dubbo's regional **museum** and **gallery** plus a lovely cafe, the cultural centre is in a swanky architectural space cleverly incorporating the main hall of Dubbo's former high school. The combination befits the centre's exhibitions, both contemporary and historic.

Old Dubbo Gaol MUSEUM
(www.olddubbogaol.com.au; 90 Macquarie St; adult/child $15/5; 9am-4pm) This is a museum where 'animatronic' characters tell their stories. There are also characters in costume and guided tours on weekends (daily in school holidays); twilight tours are possible too. Creepy but authentic.

Sleeping

There are plenty of hotels on Cobra St, and two large, family-friendly camping grounds with cabins. Although they're not cheap, the accommodation packages at Taronga Western Plains Zoo make for a night to remember.

Ibis Budget Dubbo HOTEL $
(☎ 02-6882 9211; www.ibisbudget.com; cnr Mitchell & Newell Hwys; tw/d/f $59/69/89; @) If you're simply after value for money, this is a good bet. Rooms are no-frills and compact, but come with TV, air-con and en suite. Breakfast is cheap at $7.

No 95 Dubbo MOTEL $$
(02-6882 7888; www.no95.com.au; 95 Cobra St; r $135;) Don't be put off by the uninspiring facade: inside, the rooms are equipped with top-notch furniture, linen and appliances. Facilities are first rate.

Westbury Guesthouse GUESTHOUSE $$
(02-6881 6105; www.westburydubbo.com.au; cnr Brisbane & Wingewarra Sts; s/d $125/150;) This lovely old heritage home (1915) has six spacious, elegant rooms, and a delightful Thai restaurant attached.

Eating

Village Bakery Cafe CAFE $
(www.villagebakerycafe.com.au; 113a Darling St; 6am-5.30pm;) Award-winning meat pies, sandwiches and a kids' playground make this an easy choice, helped along by cabinets full of old-school cakes and desserts.

Two Doors Tapas & Wine Bar TAPAS $$
(02-6885 2333; www.twodoors.com.au; 215 Macquarie St; dishes $7-20; 4pm-late Tue-Fri, from 10am Sat) Kick back in a leafy courtyard below street level, while munching on flavour-packed plates of haloumi skewers, soft-shell crab or slow-roasted pork belly.

Information

Visitor Centre (02-6801 4450; www.dubbo.com.au; cnr Macquarie St & Newell Hwy; 9am-5pm) At the northern end of town. Good info; bikes for hire.

Getting There & Around

Dubbo is a regional hub for transport, with major highways meeting here:

- A32 Mitchell Hwy between Sydney and Adelaide
- A39 Newell Hwy between Melbourne and Brisbane
- B84 Golden Hwy from Newcastle

Bourke

POP 2047

Bourke is one of those quintessential outback Australian towns – slow-paced and miles from anywhere. Sprawled along the Darling River, it makes for a tranquil pitstop. The reconstructed wharf at the northern end of Sturt St is impressive; see if paddle-steamer cruises on *PV Jandra* are in operation when you visit.

Sights & Activities

Back O' Bourke Exhibition Centre MUSEUM
(02-6872 1321; www.visitbourke.com.au; Kidman Way; adult/child $22/10; 9am-5pm Apr-Oct, to 4pm Mon-Fri Nov-Mar) This highly worthwhile exhibition space follows the legends of the back country (both Indigenous and settler) through interactive displays. It also houses the **Bourke visitor centre** and sells packages that include one or all of the town's major attractions – a river cruise on the *Jandra,* an entertaining outback show (staged at 11am) and a bus tour of the town and surrounds (note that the cruise and show operate April to October only).

For self-exploration, ask for the leaflet called *Back O' Bourke Mud Map Tours,* detailing walks, drives, attractions and businesses in the area, including station stays.

Bourke's Historic Cemetery CEMETERY
(Kidman Way) Bourke's fascinating cemetery is peppered with epitaphs such as 'perished in the bush'. Professor Fred Hollows, the renowned eye surgeon, is buried here.

PV Jandra BOATING
(02-6872 1321; departs Kidman's Camp; adult/child $16/10; 9am & 3pm Mon-Sat, 2.30pm Sun Apr-Oct) River trade was once Bourke's lifeline. The three-tiered **wharf** at the northern end of Sturt St is a reconstruction of the original built in 1897 and, on the river, the *PV Jandra* is a replica of an 1895 paddle steamer. Hear local history and view river bird life on its one-hour cruises.

Sleeping & Eating

Kidman's Camp CAMPGROUND, CABINS $$
(02-6872 1612; www.kidmanscamp.com.au/bourke/; Cunnamulla Rd, North Bourke; camp sites $30-34, cabins $99-139;) An excellent place to base yourself, on river frontage about 8km out of Bourke. The *Jandra* cruise departs from here, and 'Poetry on a Plate' is staged in the grounds. Plus there are gardens, swimming pools and cabins – family-sized with shared bathrooms, or comfy log cabins with bathroom, kitchenette and verandah.

Bourke Riverside Motel MOTEL $$
(02-6872 2539; www.bourkeriversidemotel.com.au; 3-13 Mitchell St; s/d from $110/125;) This rambling motel has riverside gardens and a range of well-appointed rooms and suites: some have heritage overtones and antique furniture, some have kitchen, some are family-sized. A fine choice.

★Poetry on a Plate AUSTRALIAN $$
(www.poetryonaplate.com.au; Kidman's Camp; adult/child $25/10; ⏲6.30pm Tue, Thu & Sun Apr-Oct) A heart-warmingly unique offering: a well-priced night of bush ballads and storytelling around a campfire under the stars, with a simple, slow-cooked meal and dessert to boot. Dress warmly and bring your own drinks, as well as your own camp chair and eating utensils (plate, cutlery and mug) – or pay an extra $5 to hire these.

Wilcannia

In the past, Wilcannia hasn't had a lot of love from travellers, but a couple of new businesses are happily changing opinions.

The town has a large Indigenous population, and a fine collection of old sandstone buildings dating from its heyday in the 1880s as a prosperous Darling River port.

Sleeping & Eating

★Warrawong on the Darling CAMPGROUND, MOTEL $$
(☎1300 688 225; www.warrawongonthedarling.com.au; Barrier Hwy; camp sites $20-35, d $120-140) Just east of town, this new riverside property has lush green camp sites by a billabong, plus the opportunity for bush camping. The self-contained motel units are excellent value, each with kitchenette and barbecue. Amenities are large and spotless. Cheerful managers make the place sparkle – plus there's a friendly emu named Rissole. Still to come: a restaurant-bar and waterfront cabins.

Courthouse Cafe & Gallery CAFE $
(☎08-8091 5910; www.courthouse.net.au; cnr Reid & Cleaton Sts; lunch $6-13; ⏲10am-4pm Wed-Mon) On a street lined with heritage buildings, this sweet cafe offers pit stop-worthy coffee and food (including a fine ploughman's lunch), homemade cakes and an arty bent.

Getting There & Away

Wilcannia lies about halfway between Broken Hill and Cobar, on the Barrier Hwy. The sealed road to White Cliffs is signposted just west of town.

Mungo National Park

This remote, beautiful and important place covers 278.5 sq km of the Willandra Lakes Region World Heritage Area. It is one of Australia's most accessible slices of the outback.

Lake Mungo is a dry lake and site of the oldest archaeological finds in Australia. It also has the longest continual record of Aboriginal life (the world's oldest recorded cremation site has been found here).

MANFRED GOTTSCHALK/GETTY IMAGES ©

Mungo National Park

Sights & Activities

Visitor Centre MUSEUM

(www.visitmungo.com.au) The visitor centre has displays on the park's cultural and natural history, and it's here you can pick up maps, pay park and camping fees, and enquire about tours. Next door is the Shearers' Quarters accommodation and the **Historic Woolshed**, dating from 1869 and well worth a look.

Behind the visitor centre is a recreation of the 20,000-year-old human footprints discovered in the park in 2003. These lead to the outdoor **Meeting Place**, of significance to the region's Indigenous groups.

★ **Walls of China** OUTDOORS

A 33km semicircle ('lunette') of sand dunes, the fabulous Walls of China has been created by the unceasing westerly wind. From the visitor centre a road leads across the dry lake bed to a car park, then it's a short walk to the **viewing platform**. Getting up close to the formations is the preserve of **guided tours**.

★ **Mungo Track** SCENIC DRIVE

The Mungo Track is a 70km signposted loop road around the heart of Mungo, linking the park's main attractions – you'll pass diverse landscapes, lookouts, short walks and plenty of emus and kangaroos. Although it's unsealed, in dry weather the road is generally fine for 2WD cars; in good weather (ie not too hot), mountain-bikers may be tempted.

Beyond the Walls of China parking area, the road continues to the pretty **Red Top Lookout**, which boasts fine views over the deeply eroded ravines of the lunette sand dunes. After that point, the Mungo Track is a one-way road that loops all the way back to the visitor centre.

Pick up a map from the visitor centre before setting out, and come equipped with enough petrol, a spare tyre and plenty of drinking water. You can break the journey with an overnight stay at Belah Camp.

Walking Trails

From Main Camp camping ground, there are short walks such as the Grasslands Nature Stroll and a path to Mungo Lookout.

From the visitor centre, the 2.5km **Foreshore Walk** follows the ancient shoreline of Lake Mungo, or you can walk or cycle the 10km **Pastoral Heritage Trail**, linking the old Mungo Woolshed with the remnants of the Zanci Homestead precinct built in the 1920s.

MUNGO NATIONAL PARK AT A GLANCE

When to Visit Year-round, but best April to October (summer temperatures are scorching)

Gateway Towns Mildura, Wentworth, Balranald, Broken Hill

Main Attractions Walls of China land formations; outback isolation; wildlife; Aboriginal sites

Transport Unsealed roads into the park are accessible in 2WD vehicles except after rains

Tours

Aboriginal Discovery Tours CULTURAL TOUR

(☎03-5021 8900; www.visitmungo.com.au/discovery-tours; adult/child $35/20) The NPWS conducts tours from the visitor centre led by Indigenous rangers, with the most popular option being the walk to the Walls of China. Check online for schedules: tours generally run daily in school holidays, weekends the rest of the year. Departure times depend on weather forecast, sunset time etc.

Sleeping & Eating

Camping or accommodation prices quoted do not include park visitor fees.

Barbecues and shaded picnic tables are available by the visitor centre. Unless you plan to eat all meals at Mungo Lodge, you need to be entirely self-sufficient and bring supplies from gateway towns.

Main Camp CAMPGROUND $

(adult/child $5/3) Located 2km from the visitor centre (where you self-register and pay). Free gas barbecues and pit toilets are available; flush toilets and showers are at the visitor centre. BYO drinking water.

Belah Camp CAMPGROUND $

(adult/child $5/3) Remote Belah Camp is on the eastern side of the dunes. No wood fires are allowed – BYO cooking appliances.

Shearers' Quarters HOSTEL $

(☎1300 072 757; www.visitmungo.com.au/accommodation; adult/child $30/10; ❄) The former shearers' quarters comprises five neat, good-value rooms (each sleeping up to six in various configurations; BYO bedding). Rooms share a communal kitchen and bathroom, and a barbecue area.

Mungo Lodge LODGE $$$
(☎1300 663 748; www.mungolodge.com.au; ste $199-269; ❄📶) Mungo's plushest option is an attractive (and pricey) deluxe cabin at Mungo Lodge, on the Mildura road about 4km from the park visitor centre. There are cheaper self-catering budget cabins that are quite scruffy but scheduled for an upgrade. There are also a handful of unadvertised budget beds ($20) in very basic quarters.

The lodge houses an inviting bar, lounge and restaurant area open for breakfast, lunch and dinner (mains $22 to $32). Bookings advised for meals.

Information

There's a park entry fee of $7 per vehicle per day, payable at the visitor centre.

Note: there is no mobile-phone coverage in the area.

NPWS Office (☎03-5021 8900; ⏲8.30am-4.30pm Mon-Fri) On the corner of the Sturt Hwy at Buronga, near Mildura.

Visitor Centre (☎03-5021 8900; www.visitmungo.com.au; ⏲approximately 8am-4pm)

Getting There & Away

Mungo is 110km from Mildura and 150km from Balranald on good, unsealed roads that become instantly impassable after rain – a 2WD vehicle is generally fine in dry weather. From Wentworth the route is about 150km, and the road is sealed for 100km.

The closest places selling fuel are Balranald, Mildura, Wentworth, Pooncarie and Menindee.

Ask at the tourist offices in the gateway towns to see if the roads into Mungo are open *and* accessible by 2WD. You can also phone ☎132 701 or 03-5027 5090, or check online at www.visitwentworth.com.au/Mungo-Road.aspx.

Broken Hill

POP 18,500

The massive mullock heap (of mine residue) that forms a backdrop for Broken Hill's town centre accentuates the unique character of this desert frontier town. For all its remoteness, the fine facilities and high-quality attractions can feel like an oasis somewhere close to the end of the earth. Some of the state's most impressive national parks are nearby, as is an intriguing near-ghost town, and everywhere there is an impressive spirit of community and creativity.

Broken Hill's unique historic value was recognised in 2015, when it became the first Australian city to be included on the National Heritage List. It joins 102 other sites (including the Sydney Opera House and the Great Barrier Reef) as examples of exceptional places that contribute to the national identity.

Sights & Activities

★**Line of Lode Miners Memorial** MEMORIAL, VIEWPOINT
(Federation Way; ⏲6am-9pm) FREE Teetering atop the silver skimp dump is this moving memorial with memorable views. It houses the impressively stark Cor-Ten steel memorial to the 900 miners who have died since Broken Hill first became a mining town; it's an appalling litany of gruesome deaths. To get here, travel south along Iodide St, cross the railway tracks then follow the signs.

★**Broken Hill Regional Art Gallery** GALLERY
(www.bhartgallery.com.au; 404-408 Argent St; admission by gold-coin donation; ⏲10am-5pm Mon-Fri, to 4pm Sat & Sun) This impressive gallery is housed in the beautifully restored Sully's Emporium from 1885. It's the oldest regional gallery in NSW and holds 1800 works in its permanent collection. Artists featured include Australian masters such as John Olsen, Sidney Nolan and Arthur Streeton, plus there is strong Indigenous representation.

★**Royal Flying Doctor Service** MUSEUM
(☎08-8080 3714; www.flyingdoctor.org.au/Broken-Hill-Base.html; Airport Rd; adult/child $8.50/4; ⏲9am-5pm Mon-Fri, 10am-3pm Sat & Sun) This iconic Australian institution has a visitor centre at the airport. There are stirring displays and stories of health innovation and derring-do in the service of those who live and work in remote places (note: this base serves a staggeringly vast area of 640,000 sq km). It's a real eye-opener, and the video is guaranteed to stir emotions.

★**Palace Hotel** HISTORIC BUILDING
(☎08-8088 1699; thepalacehotelbrokenhill.com.au; cnr Argent & Sulphide Sts) Star of the hit Australian movie *The Adventures of Priscilla, Queen of the Desert,* this impressive three-storey pub (1889) has an elaborate cast-iron verandah, plus wonderfully kitsch landscape murals covering almost every inch of the public areas. They're described as 'Italian Renaissance meets Outback' and were painted in the 1970s by Indigenous artist Gordon Waye. There's also a quality restaurant, accommodation and the outback essential: cold beer.

OUTBACK SUNSET IN THE LIVING DESERT

Living Desert Reserve (adult/child $5/2) One of the most memorable experiences of Broken Hill is viewing the sunset from the **Sculpture Symposium** on the highest hilltop 12km from town. The sculptures are the work of 12 international artists who carved the huge sandstone blocks on-site.

This spectacular outdoor gallery is part of the 24-sq-km Living Desert reserve, which is home to a **flora and fauna sanctuary** featuring a 2.2km Cultural Walk Trail and a 1km Flora Trail.

You can drive up to the sculpture summit, or walk up from the sanctuary (around 20 minutes). The lower car park is close to a nice barbecue and picnic area.

The reserve gates close about 30 minutes after sunset. The sanctuary's walks are accessible 9am to 5pm March to November, and 6am to 2pm December to February. Sunset times and opening hours are posted at the visitor centre.

★ Pro Hart Gallery GALLERY
(www.prohart.com.au; 108 Wyman St; adult/child $5/3; ⏲10am-5pm Mar-Nov, to 4pm Dec-Feb) Kevin 'Pro' Hart (1928–2006) was a former miner and is widely considered one of outback Australia's premier painters. His iconic work is spread over three storeys, his studio has been recreated, and there's a fascinating video presentation about his life and work. You can also admire his Rolls-Royce collection.

Albert Kersten Mining & Minerals Museum MUSEUM
(Geomuseum; cnr Bromide & Crystal Sts; adult/child $7/5; ⏲10am-4.45pm Mon-Fri, 1-4.45pm Sat & Sun) Fascinating displays (and a mind-bending video) explain how the richest lode of silver, lead and zinc in the world was formed through the aeons. Rare minerals and crystals are displayed, as well as a 42kg silver nugget and the celebrated Silver Tree, an epergne (table centrepiece) crafted from 8.5kg of pure silver in 1879.

Jack Absalom's Gallery GALLERY
(www.jackabsalom.com.au; 638 Chapple St; ⏲10am-5pm Mar-Dec) FREE Octogenarian Jack Absalom was one of the celebrated 'Brushmen of the Bush', a group of five artists that hailed from Broken Hill (Pro Hart was another member). Absalom's oil paintings (and opal collection) are on show in a purpose-built space attached to his home; his works beautifully capture the light and colour of outback landscapes.

Day Dream Mine MINE
(☎08-8088 5682; www.daydreammine.com.au; underground & surface tours adult/child $30/10; ⏲tours 10am & 11.30am) The first mines were walk-in, pick-and-shovel horrors. For an eye-opening experience, tour this historic mine (dating from the 1880s) where you squeeze down the steps with your helmet light quivering on your head. Sturdy footwear is essential. It's a scenic 13km dirt drive off the Silverton road – a total of 33km from Broken Hill.

Silver City Mint & Art Centre GALLERY
(www.silvercitymint.com.au; 66 Chloride St; adult/child $7.50/3; ⏲10am-4pm) This is home to the Big Picture, an amazing 100m-by-12m diorama of the Broken Hill outback – the work of one painter, over two years. It's certainly impressive, but also pricey, and the $2.50 charge to simply enter the gallery (really an elaborate souvenir shop) is cheeky.

★ Outback Astronomy ASTRONOMY
(☎0427 055 225; www.outbackastronomy.com.au; Racecourse Rd) Broken Hill is surrounded by desert, making it a great place to experience inky black skies and celestial splendour. This new company runs one-hour night-sky-viewing shows. The presenter points out constellations and various features visible to the naked eye, and through powerful binoculars (provided).

Viewing is from a lounge chair in the great outdoors (dress appropriately, especially in winter), at the racecourse on the northeast edge of town.

The website lists a calendar of forthcoming shows.

School of the Air SCHOOL LESSONS
(www.schoolair-p.schools.nsw.edu.au; 586 Lane St; admission $4.40; ⏲8.15am school days) For a back-to-school experience and a lesson in the outback's vastness, sit in on a class that broadcasts to kids in isolated homesteads. Bookings must be made at least a day in advance at the visitor centre. The school is closed during school holidays.

Broken Hill

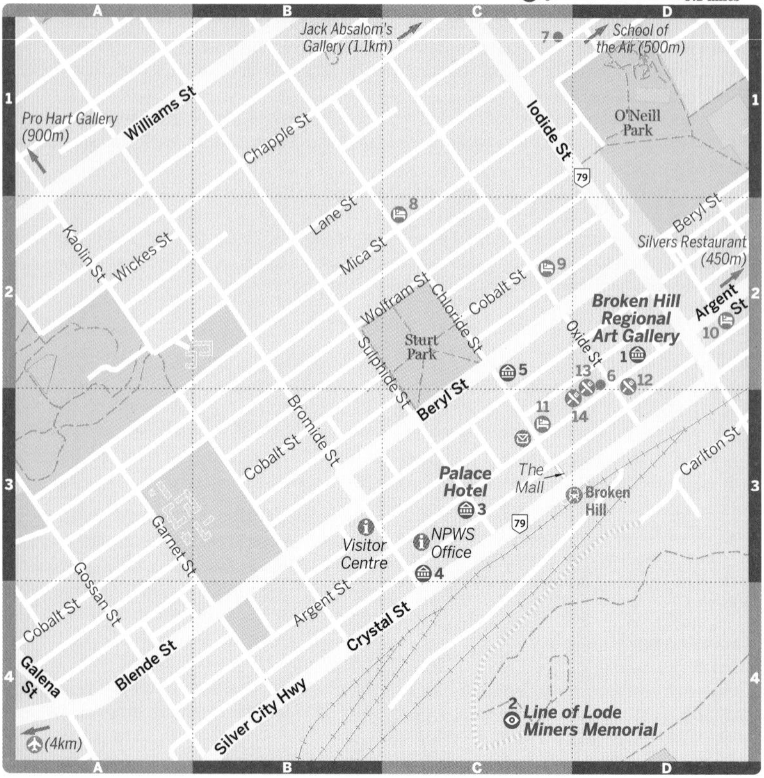

Tours

Broken Hill City Sights Tours TOUR

(08-8087 2484; www.bhoutbacktours.com.au; half-/full-day tours from $60/125) Day and half-day tours of Broken Hill, Silverton, Menindee Lakes and White Cliffs. Can transport you to Day Dream Mine. Minimum two passengers.

Silver City Tours TOUR

(08-8087 6956; www.silvercitytours.com.au; 380 Argent St) Half- and full-day tours that include Broken Hill city sights, Menindee Lakes and Kinchega National Park, White Cliffs and Silverton. Multiday packages available.

Tri State Safaris 4WD TOUR

(08-8088 2389; www.tristate.com.au; day tours $220) Well-regarded Broken Hill operator offering one- to 15-day tours to remote outback places like Mutawintji, Kinchega or Mungo National Parks, Corner Country, Birdsville and the Simpson Desert. Travellers can opt to tag-along on tours in their own 4WD vehicles.

Sleeping

★ Caledonian B&B B&B $

(08-8087 1945; www.caledonianbnb.com.au; 140 Chloride St; s/d with shared bathroom incl breakfast $79/89, cottages from $130;) This fine B&B is in a refurbished pub (1898) known as 'the Cally' – it also has three self-contained cottages, each sleeping up to six. Hugh and Barb are welcoming hosts and the rooms are lovingly maintained. Wake up and smell Hugh's espresso coffee and you'll be hooked.

Palace Hotel HISTORIC HOTEL $

(08-8088 1699; www.thepalacehotelbrokenhill.com.au; 227 Argent St; dm/s/d with shared bathroom from $30/45/65, d $115-135;) This huge and ageing icon won't be to everyone's taste, but a stay here is one of the outback's most unique sleeping experiences. There are newer rooms with balcony access and en suite, but most rooms are proudly retro and the murals in the public areas are extraordinary. For the full experience, try the Priscilla Suite ($135).

Broken Hill

Top Sights

1 Broken Hill Regional Art Gallery D2
2 Line of Lode Miners Memorial C4
3 Palace Hotel C3

Sights

4 Albert Kersten Mining & Minerals Museum C3
5 Silver City Mint & Art Centre C2

Activities, Courses & Tours

6 Silver City Tours D2
7 Tri State Safaris C1

Sleeping

8 Caledonian B&B C2
9 Imperial C2
Palace Hotel .... (see 3)
10 Red Earth Motel D2
11 Royal Exchange Hotel C3

Eating

12 Café Alfresco D2
13 Silly Goat D2
14 Thom, Dick & Harry's D3

Drinking & Nightlife

Palace Hotel .... (see 3)

★**Red Earth Motel** MOTEL $$
(☎08-8088 5694; www.redearthmotel.com.au; 469 Argent St; studio apt $160, 2-/3-bedroom apt $220/260;) One of the best motels in rural NSW, this outstanding family-run place has large, stylish rooms.

Imperial GUESTHOUSE $$
(☎08-8087 7444; www.imperialfineaccommodation.com; 88 Oxide St; r/apt incl breakfast from $170/270;) One of Broken Hill's best, this converted heritage pub, with a spectacular wrought-iron verandah, has been graciously renovated and has all the creature comforts.

Royal Exchange Hotel HOTEL $$
(☎08-8087 2308; www.royalexchangehotel.com; 320 Argent St; r $135-180;) This restored 1930s hotel with an art-deco bent is an accommodation oasis in the heart of town.

Eating & Drinking

★**Silly Goat** CAFE $
(360 Argent St; dishes $8-16; 7.30am-5pm Tue-Fri, 8am-2pm Sat, 8am-1pm Sun) What's this? Pour-overs and single-origin coffee in the outback? Nice work, Silly Goat. The menu here would be at home in any big-city cafe, the array of cakes is tempting, the coffee is great, and the vibe is busy and cheerful.

Bells Milk Bar MILK BAR $
(www.bellsmilkbar.com.au; 160 Patton St; snacks $4-7; 10am-5.30pm;) In South Broken Hill (follow Crystal St west from the train station), this glorious old milk bar is a slice of 1950s nostalgia. Sip on a 'soda spider' or milkshake and soak up the memorabilia from one of the Formica tables.

Thom, Dick & Harry's CAFE $
(thomdickharrys.com.au; 354 Argent St; baguettes $8.50; 8am-5.30pm Mon-Thu, to 6pm Fri, 9am-2pm Sat) A narrow shop cluttered with stylish kitchenware and gourmet produce. Sit in among it (or out on the street) for a decent coffee and delicious baguette.

Silvers Restaurant INTERNATIONAL $$
(☎08-8088 4380; cnr Argent & Silver Sts; mains $25-37; from 6pm Mon-Sat) It's not cheap, but the unassuming restaurant at the Junction Hotel offers a surprise: tucked among the traditional classics is a selection of tasty curry dishes. Service is good, and the dessert trolley is a fine retro touch.

Café Alfresco MODERN AUSTRALIAN $$
(397 Argent St; dinner mains $15-29; 7am-late) The service ticks along at an outback pace but this all-day place pulls an unfussy local crowd pining for its bumper portions of meat dishes (classics like steak and chicken parma) or crowd-pleasing pizza and pasta.

★**Palace Hotel** PUB
(☎08-8088 1699; thepalacehotelbrokenhill.com.au; 227 Argent St; from 3pm Mon-Wed, from noon Thu-Sat) In a town with *dozens* of pubs, it's hard to go past the storied Palace for true-blue outback entertainment. There's good food in the **Sidebar restaurant** (mains $17 to $36), drinks and snacks on the 1st-floor balcony, occasional live music, and on Fridays you can play 'two-up' (gambling on the fall of two coins) from 9pm.

Information

NPWS Office (☎08-8080 3200; 183 Argent St; 8.30am-4.30pm Mon-Fri) National park information, road-closure updates and park accommodation bookings.

Visitor Centre (☎08-8088 3560; www.visitbrokenhill.com.au; cnr Blende & Bromide Sts; 8.30am-5pm Mar-Nov, to 3pm Dec-Feb)

Driving in Australia

With more than 350,000km of paved roads criss-crossing the country, Australia is an infinitely fascinating road movie come to life.

Driving Fast Facts

- **Right or left?** Drive on the left
- **Blood alcohol concentration limit** 0.05 (0.00 for learners and probationary drivers)
- **Signature car** Holden Commodore

DRIVING LICENCE & DOCUMENTS

To drive in Australia you'll need to hold a current driving licence issued in English from your home country. If the licence isn't in English, you'll also need to carry an International Driving Permit, issued in your home country.

INSURANCE

Third-party insurance With the exception of NSW and Queensland, third-party personal-injury insurance is included in the vehicle registration cost, ensuring that every registered vehicle carries at least minimum insurance (if registering your own car in NSW or Queensland, you'll need to arrange this privately). We recommend extending that minimum to at least third-party property insurance – minor collisions can be amazingly expensive.

Rental vehicles When it comes to hire cars, understand your liability in the event of an accident. Rather than risk paying out thousands of dollars, consider taking out comprehensive car insurance or paying an additional daily amount to the rental company for excess reduction (this reduces the excess payable in the event of an accident from between $2000 and $5000 to a few hundred dollars).

Exclusions Be aware that if travelling on dirt roads, you usually will not be covered by insurance unless you have a 4WD (read the fine print). Also, many companies' insurance won't cover the cost of damage to glass (including the windscreen) or tyres.

HIRING A CAR

Larger car-rental companies have drop-offs in major cities and towns. Most companies require drivers to be over the age of 21, though in some cases it's 18 and in others 25.

Suggestions to assist in the process:

- Read the contract from cover to cover.
- Some companies may require a signed credit-card slip as a bond, others may actually charge your credit card; if this is the case, find out when you'll get a refund.
- Ask if unlimited kilometres are included and, if not, what the extra charge per kilometre is.

Road Trip Websites

Australian Bureau of Meteorology (www.bom.gov.au) Weather information.

Department of Planning, Transport & Infrastructure (☎1300 361 033; www.transport.sa.gov.au) SA road conditions.

Green Vehicle Guide (www.greenvehicleguide.gov.au) Rates Australian vehicles based on greenhouse and air-pollution emissions.

Live Traffic NSW (☎1300 131 122; www.livetraffic.com) NSW road conditions.

Main Roads Western Australia (☎13 81 38; www.mainroads.wa.gov.au) WA road conditions.

Motorcycle Council of NSW (☎1300 679 622; www.mccofnsw.org.au) One of many such organisations around Australia.

Road Report (☎1800 246 199; www.roadreport.nt.gov.au) NT road conditions.

Traffic & Travel Information (☎13 19 40; www.transport.sa.gov.au) Queensland road conditions.

➡ Find out what excess you'll have to pay if you have a prang, and if it can be lowered by an extra charge per day (this option will usually be offered to you whether you ask or not). Check if your personal travel insurance covers you for vehicle accidents and excess.

➡ Check for exclusions (hitting a kangaroo, damage on unsealed roads etc) and whether you're covered on unavoidable unsealed roads (eg accessing camp sites). Some companies also exclude parts of the car from cover, such as the underbelly, tyres and windscreen.

➡ At pick-up inspect the vehicle for any damage. Make a note of anything on the contract before you sign.

➡ Ask about breakdown and accident procedures.

➡ If you can, return the vehicle during business hours and insist on an inspection in your presence.

The usual big international companies operate in Australia (Avis, Budget, Europcar, Hertz, Thrifty). The following websites offer last-minute discounts and the opportunity to compare rates between the big operators:

➡ www.carhire.com.au

➡ www.drivenow.com.au

➡ www.webjet.com.au

MAPS

Good-quality road and topographical maps are plentiful and readily available around Australia. State motoring organisations are a dependable source of road maps, including road atlases with comprehensive coverage of road networks.

Hema's *Australia Road Atlas* is a good general road atlas covering the entire country, and it also offers a range of smaller fold-out maps on specific destinations.

ROADS & CONDITIONS

Australia's roads are generally in excellent condition, but never discount the possibility of potholes, especially in rural areas that receive heavy truck traffic.

Overtaking Lanes

If you've spent any time in Europe, you'll be underwhelmed by Australia's dearth of dual carriageway roads. Apart from the Hume Fwy connecting Sydney and Melbourne (the inland route, not the coast road), most motorways are restricted to a 100km (or less) radius around major cities. Although there are regular overtaking lanes on many roads and traffic flows generally maintain a reasonable speed, there are times when you'll become frustrated as you wait to pass a slow caravan, truck or old man in a hat out for a Sunday drive. The only sensible response in such circumstances is patience.

Unsealed Roads

At last count, Australia was so vast that it had 466,874km of unsealed roads – that's significantly more than the distance from earth to the moon! While many of these are suitable for 2WD vehicles when conditions are dry, many more are not, and most become treacherous or impassable after even a little rain. Others peter out into the sand. The simple rule is this – never leave the paved road unless you know the road, have checked recent weather conditions and asked locals for their advice.

Toll Roads

Toll roads are restricted to freeways within major cities such as Melbourne and Sydney. If you're travelling in a rental vehicle, it should have the necessary electronic reader and any tolls will be charged when you return your vehicle. Either way, take note of any numbers to call at the tollpoints to make sure you don't get hit with a fine for late payment – you usually have between one and three days to make any payment.

ROAD RULES

Give way An important road rule is 'give way to the right' – if an intersection is unmarked (unusual) and at roundabouts, you must give way to vehicles entering the intersection from your right.

Speed limits The general speed limit in built-up and residential areas is 50km/h. Near schools, the limit is usually 25km/h (sometimes 40km/h) in the morning and afternoon. On the highway it's usually 100km/h or 110km/h; in the NT it's either 110km/h or 130km/h. Police have speed radar guns and cameras and are fond of using them in strategic locations.

Seatbelts and car seats It's the law to wear seatbelts in the front and back seats; you're likely to get a fine if you don't. Small children must be belted into an approved safety seat.

Drink-driving Random breath-tests are common. If you're caught with a blood-alcohol level of more than 0.05% expect a fine and the loss of your licence. Police can randomly pull any driver over for a breathalyser or drug test.

Mobile phones Using a mobile phone while driving is illegal in Australia (excluding hands-free technology).

FUEL

Fuel types Unleaded and diesel fuel is available from service stations sporting well-known international brand names. LPG (liquefied petroleum gas) is not always stocked at more remote roadhouses; if you're on gas it's safer to have dual-fuel capacity.

Costs Prices vary from place to place, but at the time of writing unleaded was hovering

Driving Problem-Buster

What should I do if my car breaks down? Call the service number of your car-hire company and a local garage will be contacted.

What if I have an accident? Your first call should be to the insurance company and you should make sure that you have the contact details (at the very least) of the drivers of all other vehicles involved. Never admit fault unless instructed to do so by your insurance company. For minor accidents you'll need to fill out an accident statement when you return the vehicle. If problems crop up, go to the nearest police station.

What should I do if I get stopped by the police? The police will want to see your driving licence, passport (if you're from overseas) and proof of insurance.

What if I can't find anywhere to stay? If you're travelling during summer and/or holiday periods, always book accommodation in advance as beds fill up fast. If you're stuck and it's getting late, motels and motor inns line the roadside in even small Australian towns, while in outback areas the nearest roadhouse (a one-stop shop for accommodation, food and fuel) is likely to be your only option.

Road Distances (km)

	Adelaide	Albany	Alice Springs	Birdsville	Brisbane	Broome	Cairns	Canberra	Cape York	Darwin	Kalgoorlie	Melbourne	Perth	Sydney	Townsville
Albany	2649														
Alice Springs	1512	3573													
Birdsville	1183	3244	1176												
Brisbane	1942	4178	1849	1573											
Broome	4043	2865	2571	3564	5065										
Cairns	3079	5601	2396	1919	1705	4111									
Canberra	1372	4021	2725	2038	1287	5296	2923								
Cape York	4444	6566	3361	2884	2601	5076	965	3888							
Darwin	3006	5067	1494	2273	3774	1844	2820	3948	3785						
Kalgoorlie	2168	885	3092	2763	3697	3052	5234	3540	6199	4896					
Melbourne	728	3377	2240	1911	1860	4811	3496	637	4461	3734	2896				
Perth	2624	411	3548	3219	4153	2454	6565	3996	7530	4298	598	3352			
Sydney	1597	4246	3109	2007	940	5208	2634	289	3599	3917	3765	862	3869		
Townsville	3237	5374	2055	1578	1295	3770	341	2582	1306	2479	4893	3155	5349	2293	
Uluru	1559	3620	441	1617	2290	3012	2837	2931	3802	1935	3139	2287	3595	2804	2496

	Bicheno	Cradle Mountain	Devonport	Hobart	Launceston
Cradle Mountain	383				
Devonport	283	100			
Hobart	186	296	334		
Launceston	178	205	105	209	
Queenstown	443	69	168	257	273

These are the shortest distances by road; other routes may be considerably longer. For distances by coach, check the companies' leaflets.

between $1.20 and $1.50 in the cities. Out in the country, prices soar – in outback NT, SA, WA and Queensland you can pay as much as $2.20 per litre.

Availability In cities and towns petrol stations proliferate, but distances between fill-ups can be long in the outback. That said, there are only a handful of tracks where you'll require a long-range fuel tank. On main roads there'll be a small town or roadhouse roughly every 150km to 200km. Many petrol stations, but not all, are open 24 hours.

SAFETY

Theft from vehicles can be an issue in large cities or tourist areas, but the risk is unlikely to be any higher than you'd encounter back home.

Animal Hazards

➡ Roadkill is a huge problem in Australia and many Australians avoid travelling once the sun drops because of the risks posed by nocturnal animals on the roads.

➡ Kangaroos are common on country roads, as are cows and sheep in the unfenced outback. Kangaroos are most active around dawn and dusk and often travel in groups: if you see one hopping across the road, slow right down, as its friends may be just behind it.

➡ If you hit and kill an animal while driving, pull it off the road, preventing the next car from having a potential accident. If the animal is only injured and is small, or perhaps an orphaned joey (baby kangaroo), wrap it in a towel or blanket and call the relevant wildlife rescue line:

Department of Environment & Heritage Protection (☎1300 264 625; www.ehp.qld.gov.au) Queensland.

Department of Parks & Wildlife (Wildcare Helpline ☎08-9474 9055; www.parks.dpaw.wa.gov.au) WA.

Fauna Rescue of South Australia (☎08-7226 0017; www.faunarescue.org.au) SA.

NSW Wildlife Information, Rescue & Education Service (WIRES; ☎1300 094 737; www.wires.org.au) NSW.

Parks & Wildlife Service (after hours ☎03-6165 4305, 1300 827 727; www.parks.tas.gov.au) Tasmania.

Wildcare Inc NT (☎0408 885 341, 08-8988 6121; www.wildcarent.org.au) NT.

Wildlife Victoria (☎1300 094 535; www.wildlifevictoria.org.au) Victoria.

Behind the Wheel

Fatigue Be wary of driver fatigue; driving long distances (particularly in hot weather) can be utterly exhausting. Falling asleep at the wheel is not uncommon. On a long haul, stop and rest every two hours or so – do some exercise, change drivers or have a coffee.

Road trains Be careful when overtaking road trains (trucks with two or three trailers stretching for as long as 50m); you'll need distance and plenty of speed. On single-lane roads get right off the road when one approaches.

Unsealed roads Unsealed road conditions vary wildly and cars perform differently when braking and turning on dirt. Don't exceed 80km/h on dirt roads; if you go faster, you won't have time to respond to a sharp turn, stock on the road or an unmarked gate or cattle grid.

OUTBACK DRIVING

In 'Power & the Passion', Midnight Oil's damning ode to the Australian suburban condition, Peter Garrett sings, 'And no one goes outback that's that.' It really is amazing how few Australians have explored the outback. To many, it's either a mythical place inhabited by tourists and Indigenous Australians, or something for the too-hard basket – too hot, too far to drive, too expensive to fly, too many sand dunes and flies... But for those who make the effort, a strange awakening occurs – a quiet comprehension of the primal terrain and profound size of Australia that you simply can't fathom while sitting on Bondi Beach.

About the Outback

The Australian outback is vast, blanketing the centre of the continent. While most Australians live on the coast, that thin green fringe of the continent is hardly typical of this enormous land mass. Inland is the desert soul of Australia.

Weather patterns vary from region to region – from sandy arid deserts to semi-arid scrublands to tropical savannah – but you can generally rely on hot sunny days, starry night skies and mile after mile of unbroken horizon.

Australia Playlist

'Flame Trees' (Cold Chisel; 1984) Small town, big song.

'Back In Black' (AC/DC; 1980) The greatest guitar riff ever?

'Wide Open Road' (The Triffids; 1986) Road-tripping melancholia.

'Beds Are Burning' (Midnight Oil; 1987) Aboriginal land rights anthem. Any Midnight Oil would be a fine thing to have in your glove box.

'Under The Milky Way' (The Church; 1988) Arty haircuts, pointy shoes, jangly guitars.

'Nullarbor' (Kasey Chambers; 2010) Poignant understatement from Australia's first lady of alt-country.

Great albums to have on hand are:

- *Diesel & Dust* (Midnight Oil)
- *Circus Animals* (Cold Chisel)
- *Neon Ballroom* (Silverchair)
- *Kick* (INXS)
- *Woodface* (Crowded House)
- *The Boatman's Call* (Nick Cave & the Bad Seeds)
- *Songs From the South: Paul Kelly's Greatest Hits* (Paul Kelly)

Type of Vehicle

2WD Depending on where you want to travel, a regulation 2WD vehicle might suffice. They're cheaper to hire, buy and run than 4WDs and are more readily available. Most are fuel efficient, and easy to repair and sell. Downsides: no off-road capability and no room to sleep!

4WD Four-wheel drives are good for outback travel as they can access almost any track you get a hankering for. And there might even be space to sleep in the back. Downsides: poor fuel economy, awkward to park and more expensive to hire or buy.

Campervan Creature comforts at your fingertips: sink, fridge, cupboards, beds, kitchen and space to relax. Downsides: slow and often not fuel-efficient, not great on dirt roads and too big for nipping around the city.

Motorcycle The Australian climate is great for riding, and bikes are handy in city traffic. Downsides: Australia isn't particularly bike-friendly in terms of driver awareness, there's limited luggage capacity, and exposure to the elements.

Outback Driving & Safety Checklist

You need to be particularly organised and vigilant when travelling in the outback, especially on remote sandy tracks, due to the scorching temperatures, long distances between fuel stops and isolation. Following are a few tips.

Communication

➡ Report your route and schedule to the police, a friend or relative.

➡ Mobile phones are practically useless in the outback. A safety net is to hire a satellite phone, high-frequency (HF) radio transceiver equipped to pick up the Royal Flying Doctor Service bases, or emergency position-indicating radio beacon (EPIRB).

➡ In an emergency, stay with your vehicle; it's easier to spot than you are, and you won't be able to carry a heavy load of water very far. Don't sit inside your vehicle as it will become an oven in hot weather.

➡ If you do become stranded, set fire to a spare tyre (let the air out first). The pall of smoke will be visible for miles.

Dirt-Road Driving

➡ Inflate your tyres to the recommended levels for the terrain you're travelling on; on desert dirt, deflate your tyres to 25psi to avoid punctures.

➡ Reduce speed on unsealed roads, as traction is decreased and braking distances increase.

Road Trains

On many outback highways you'll see thundering road trains: huge trucks (a prime mover plus two or three trailers) up to 50m long. These things don't move over for anyone, and it's like a scene out of *Mad Max* having one bear down on you at 120km/h. When you see a road train approaching on a narrow bitumen road, slow down and pull over – if the truck has to put its wheels off the road to pass you, the resulting barrage of stones will almost certainly smash your windscreen. When trying to overtake one, allow plenty of room (about a kilometre) to complete the manoeuvre. Road trains throw up a lot of dust on dirt roads, so if you see one coming it's best to just pull over and stop until it's gone past.

And while you're on outback roads, don't forget to give the standard bush wave to oncoming drivers – it's simply a matter of lifting the index finger off the steering wheel to acknowledge your fellow motorist.

Automobile Associations

Under the auspices of the **Australian Automobile Association** (☎02-6247 7311; www.aaa.asn.au) are automobile clubs in each state, handy when it comes to insurance, regulations, maps and roadside assistance. Club membership (around $100 to $150) can save you a lot of trouble if things go wrong mechanically. If you're a member of an auto club in your home country, check if reciprocal rights are offered in Australia. The major Australian auto clubs generally offer reciprocal rights in other states and territories.

AANT (Automobile Association of the Northern Territory; ☎13 11 11; www.aant.com.au)

NRMA (National Roads & Motorists' Association; ☎13 11 22; www.mynrma.com.au) NSW and the ACT.

RAC (Royal Automobile Club of Western Australia; ☎13 17 03; www.rac.com.au)

RACQ (Royal Automobile Club of Queensland; ☎13 19 05; www.racq.com.au)

RACT (Royal Automobile Club of Tasmania; ☎13 27 22; www.ract.com.au)

RACV (Royal Automobile Club of Victoria; ☎13 72 28; www.racv.com.au)

➡ Dirt roads are often corrugated: keeping an even speed is the best approach.

➡ Dust on outback roads can obscure your vision, so always stop and wait for it to settle.

➡ If your vehicle is struggling through deep sand, deflating your tyres a bit will help. If you do get stuck, don't attempt to get out by revving the engine; this just causes wheels to dig in deeper.

Road Hazards

➡ Outback highways are usually long, flat ribbons of tarmac stretching across the red desert flats. The temptation is to get it over with quickly, but try to keep a lid on your speed.

➡ Take a rest every few hours: driver fatigue is a real problem.

➡ Wandering cattle, sheep, emus, kangaroos, camels etc make driving fast a dangerous prospect. Take care and avoid nocturnal driving, as this is often when native animals come out. Many car-hire companies prohibit night-time driving.

➡ Road trains are an ever-present menace on the main highways. Give them a wide berth – they're much bigger than you!

Supplies & Equipment

➡ Always carry plenty of water: in warm weather allow 5L per person per day and an extra amount for the radiator, carried in several containers.

➡ Bring plenty of food in case of a breakdown.

➡ Carry a first-aid kit, a good set of maps, a torch and spare batteries, a compass, and a shovel for digging if you get bogged.

Weather & Road Conditions

➡ Check road conditions before travelling: roads that are passable in the Dry (March to October) can disappear beneath water during the Wet.

➡ Check weather forecasts daily.

➡ Keep an eye out for potholes, rough sections, roads changing surfaces without notice, soft and broken verges, and single-lane bridges.

➡ Take note of the water-level markers at creek crossings to gauge the water's depth before you proceed.

➡ Don't attempt to cross flooded bridges or causeways unless you're sure of the depth, and of any road damage hidden underwater.

Your Vehicle

➡ Have your vehicle serviced and checked before you leave.

➡ Load your vehicle evenly, with heavy items inside and light items on the roof rack.

➡ Check locations and opening times of service stations, and carry spare fuel and provisions; opportunities for fill-ups can be infrequent.

➡ Carry essential tools: a spare tyre (two if possible), a fan belt and a radiator hose, as well as a tyre-pressure gauge and an air pump.

➡ An off-road jack might come in handy, as will a snatchem strap or tow rope for quick extraction when you're stuck (useful if there's another vehicle to pull you out).

➡ A set of cheap, high-profile tyres (around $80 each) will give your car a little more ground clearance.

BEHIND THE SCENES

SEND US YOUR FEEDBACK

We love to hear from travellers – your comments help make our books better. We read every word, and we guarantee that your feedback goes straight to the authors. Visit **lonelyplanet.com/contact** to submit your updates and suggestions.

Note: We may edit, reproduce and incorporate your comments in Lonely Planet products such as guidebooks, websites and digital products, so let us know if you don't want your comments reproduced or your name acknowledged. For a copy of our privacy policy visit lonelyplanet.com/privacy.

ACKNOWLEDGMENTS

Climate map data adapted from Peel MC, Finlayson BL & McMahon TA (2007) 'Updated World Map of the Köppen-Geiger Climate Classification', *Hydrology and Earth System Sciences*, 11, 163344.

Cover photographs: Front: Uluru, Northern Territory, HP Huber/4Corners; Back: Kata Tjuta (The Olgas), Northern Territory, Peter Adams/AWL

THIS BOOK

This 1st edition of *Outback Australia Road Trips* was researched and written by Anthony Ham, Carolyn Bain, Alan Murphy, Charles Rawlings-Way and Meg Worby. This guidebook was produced by the following:

Destination Editor Tasmin Waby

Product Editor Martine Power

Senior Cartographer Julie Sheridan

Cartographer Diana Von Holdt

Book Designer Jessica Rose

Assisting Editor Anne Mulvaney

Cover Researcher Campbell McKenzie

Thanks to Shahara Ahmed, Sasha Baskett, Kate Chapman, Brendan Dempsey, James Hardy, Indra Kilfoyle, Katherine Marsh, Anne Mason, Kate Mathews, Wibowo Rusli, Diana Saengkham, Angela Tinson, Amanda Williamson

OUR STORY

A beat-up old car, a few dollars in the pocket and a sense of adventure. In 1972 that's all Tony and Maureen Wheeler needed for the trip of a lifetime – across Europe and Asia overland to Australia. It took several months, and at the end – broke but inspired – they sat at their kitchen table writing and stapling together their first travel guide, *Across Asia on the Cheap*. Within a week they'd sold 1500 copies. Lonely Planet was born.

Today, Lonely Planet has offices in Melbourne, London and Oakland, with more than 600 staff and writers. We share Tony's belief that 'a great guidebook should do three things: inform, educate and amuse'.

INDEX

000 Map pages

000 Map pages

T

U

V

W

Y

Z

000 Map pages

MEG WORBY

In researching this title, this was Meg's 780th re-entry into her most habitable home state of South Australia. She is a former member of Lonely Planet's languages, editorial, web and publishing teams in Melbourne and London.

OUR WRITERS

ANTHONY HAM

Anthony was born in Melbourne, grew up in Sydney and has spent much of his adult life travelling the world. He recently returned to Australia after 10 years living in Madrid and brings to this guide more than 15 years' experience as a travel writer. As a recently returned expat, Anthony is loving the opportunity to rediscover his country and indulge his passion for wilderness. He brings to the book the unique perspective of knowing the land intimately and yet seeing it anew as if through the eyes of an outsider. Check out his website, anthonyham.com.

ALAN MURPHY

Alan has travelled extensively across Australia and worked on several Australian guidebook titles for Lonely Planet. The Northern Territory, with its ancient landscapes, outback characters and Indigenous culture holds a special place in his heart. On this research trip he criss-crossed the enormous expanse of the Territory and loved discovering new places. Alan has also written several online articles on the NT's Indigenous Australians and feels privileged to have had the opportunity of learning more about their culture on this trip.

CAROLYN BAIN

Every summer of her childhood, Carolyn's family whizzed through regional NSW (twice) on the 3500km return journey from their home near Melbourne to the beaches of the Gold Coast. On this research trip Carolyn had considerably more time to explore, and covered 6500km of glorious NSW scenery under big blue skies, from the scorching sands of Mungo to the vineyards of Mudgee. The outback's 40°C temps made a change from her usual travel-writing stomping grounds of Iceland and Denmark. Read more at carolynbain.com.au.

CHARLES RAWLINGS-WAY

As a likely lad, Charles suffered in shorts through Tasmanian winters, and in summer counted the days til he visited his grandparents in Adelaide. With desert-hot days, cool swimming pools and four TV stations, this flat city held paradisiacal status. Charles has penned 20-something Lonely Planet guidebooks.

MORE WRITERS

Published by Lonely Planet Publications Pty Ltd
ABN 36 005 607 983
1st edition – November 2015
ISBN 978 1 74360 944 6

10 9 8 7 6 5 4 3 2 1
Printed in China